D1547139

Stop Boring Me!

How to Create Kick-Ass Marketing Content, Products and Ideas
Through the Power of Improv

Kathy Klotz-Guest

DEDICATION

This book is dedicated to my hubby who reminds me why I work hard.
I called him once when we were dating and said, "I have a crazy idea."
After I finished explaining, he responded, "That's one of the most
ridiculous things I've heard. You must do it!" That's why I love him and
our beautiful son, madly.

CONTENTS

ACKNOWLEDGMENTS

I'd like to acknowledge the following people for their continued support: my patient husband; my beautiful son, who is still my favorite audience; my improv group, *Make Your Own Damn Sandwich*, and my smart, funny, and talented Harold Team at Pear Theatre—both of whom make me laugh until I pee my pants; and to my amazing friends and colleagues who asked relentlessly and patiently with love, "Where the hell is your book?" Now I can answer that. You hold me to a high standard. I hope I've hit that standard here.

INTRODUCTION:
185 MARKETERS WALK
INTO A BAR

Welcome!

First, I want to give you a heartfelt "thank you" for buying this book and investing your time in it. I hope it gives you great ideas, makes you smile, helps you to look at content and storytelling in new ways, and banishes boring from your marketing. Your audience wants to be inspired, entertained, and educated. I know you care about that, too.

Source: gratisography.com

Big Marketing Challenges: Humanity and Connection

I wrote this book because content, storytelling, and marketing in general need a shot of creativity, humanity, and fun if they are going to get results for your business. Together, we're going to eradicate boring, superficial storytelling and bad content. Sadly, there is too little meaningful content today. It's a case of too much ineffective content chasing too little (and over-saturated) customer mindshare.

In its most recent survey, the Content Marketing Institute[i] listed generating new content among the biggest challenges businesses of all sizes face. In the work I do with organizations, I see many of the same "stuckness." The challenge is more than just content ideas and volume of content. Marketing teams sometimes forget how to add human elements in their storytelling and content that would make a world of difference in connecting with audiences. Most business storytelling and content reads like a transaction rather than a conversation with emotion. Creating storytelling and content with an emotional 'punch' that gets people to act can be tricky, both in crafting the right types and amounts. We all feel content overload. There is no easy app to fix that.

Like many content marketers, or marketers in general, you, too, may be hitting a wall—and not one of those fun climbing walls—coming up with fresh, engaging ideas. Or you may wish to humanize your storytelling by giving it more emotional resonance, which makes a difference in engagement *and* sales. No sale starts without a connection. Connect with the rational *and* emotional centers of your buyers' brains and you'll sell more.

Marketers spend a great deal of money on PPC (pay per click) and SEO (search engine optimization), content distribution, tools to manage our social posts, and data analytics—all important, technical parts to content management. Yet, how much time and money do marketers spend on creating content that inspires, helps, and engages people? Too often, organizations throw technology at the content issue and end up scaling ineffective content.

We have to start with really great content.

Source: Keepingithuman.com

Back away from the content calendar, grab a cup of coffee, and let's look at content in a different, much more creative way. Improv methods increase the fun, utility and humanity quotients in our marketing, and allow us to see things in fresh ways when we need it most. When content is at its best, it produces results by grabbing something visceral in your reader so they share it and eventually contact you. I believe improv-powered techniques can help get us closer to creating the kinds of content audiences want and marketers want to produce. No kid ever says, "I want to grow up and create boring content for a living!" Your inner kid wants to play and be creative. Your audience's inner kids want that, too.

Who This Book is For

This book is written primarily for marketing, content marketing, sales, and branding people, as well as for entrepreneurs who must:

- Tell stories in business (internally, externally, when looking for funding as a startup or entrepreneur, throughout the sales process to demonstrate that companies understand and have experience successfully resolving specific customer challenges, to close business, to create change – any business, branding and marketing storytelling)
- Generate bold content and content ideas (and innovate product and service ideas, too) consistently (for yourself and for others)
- Present, sell, and advocate big ideas in exciting ways (read: not boring and self-serving) to engage audiences

The bottom line: engaging content connects with people emotionally and moves people to take action.

Even if you don't work in marketing, sales, or product, you are a creative storyteller. Each of us has that spark. We are all creative. You can use the exercises and examples in this book to come up with new ideas for products, content and for better stories! I've used these exercises with engineering and HR teams, too. Improvisation elements will not only make you more creative, they will make you a better communicator and connector. And these approaches are fun. And fun is a creative catalyst. Improv is like zesty Sriracha sauce (or substitute your favorite sauce here) for creativity.

Defining Improv: It Boils Down to Playfulness

Improvisation connects. It takes us on an emotional journey that makes us care because we see the humanity at the center of the stories being told, and fun in the games being played. Additionally, improvisation is fabulous for sparking new ideas.

Source: gratisography.com

Although there are many varieties, improvisation boils down to two basic categories:

Short-form: short games that pop in a big laugh at 3-5 minutes (and deliver laughs all through-out a scene). You've seen this type of improvisation if you have watched the popular television show, *"Whose Line is it, Anyway?"* These games can be used to generate massively creative content and marketing ideas.

Long-form: fully improvised, longer plays. Based on audience suggestions and games played out by the participants, improvisers create 30-45 minute (or longer) pieces. Long-form improvisation is not always "comedy" as you would see in short-form. Often, in long-form you see the full spectrum of human emotions and expressions—happy, hilarious, poignant, sad, ebullient, for example. The focus in long-form is portraying characters in real ways. Long-form improv works great for inspiring longer marketing storytelling pieces, also called "long-form content." Coincidence? Ok, maybe.

And some improvisers even refer to a hybrid in length called "mid-form."

All storytelling is about emotional truth. The deeper and more vulnerable you are with your truth, the more meaningful your connection with your audience will be. So if you ask me how to create a better story, I'll ask you, "what's at the core of your emotional truth?" *That's* the glue that bonds.

KATHY KLOTZ-GUEST
KEEPINGITHUMAN.COM

Source: Keepingithuman.com

You might be thinking, "Oh, great. Improv is theatricality. How the heck can I use it? Isn't it risky?"

Improv is not about theatricality. It's about being playful. No content-generating strategy is risk-free, and using improvisation to bolster your storytelling and content creation isn't inherently more risky. If we capture that human truth and emotional resonance in our stories, we will connect more meaningfully with content-weary audiences who are hungry for good stuff.

This book is not about being funny, per se, although it *is* about fun. You can't get to funny without fun. Try spelling it! Humor isn't about trying hard to be funny. Really. Humor is about truth. Like comedy, business storytelling and content work best when they are focused on the truths your audiences face. Great information that is of high utility and packaged in a fun way (and funny where you can be) is a boring-busting formula. *Comedy nerd side note*: I do define comedy differently from humor and fun. Here I bundle them together for simplicity and because most people, like my mom, don't really care about the nuances like I do.

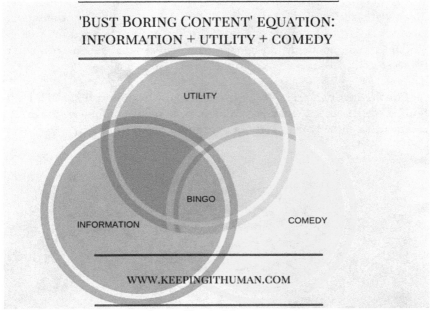

Source: Keepingithuman.com

You don't have to be a stage improviser to see new possibilities for your content marketing with improv-based approaches. You are already a business improviser, and a creative storyteller; improv techniques are designed to help you unleash more of that creativity. You and your team can use word associations, mind-mapping, scene-heightening tricks, and all of the methods improvisers use in scene work onstage to create better content. It's creativity, fun, playfulness, and humor in a bottle. Or, in this case, book! Improv is circuit training for your creative brain.

Don't give up if it takes you a few passes to get the hang of some of these ideas. Some concepts will come quickly. Others take practice.

My Creative, Risk-Taking Journey Through Improv

I have been performing comedy and improvisation for about 20 years. I started in stand-up and sketch comedy, so I was used to lots of writing and re-writing. I wrote and practiced my content so I had a "set list" down tight and tested jokes before I hit the stage. For improvisation, however, I had to be in my gut, not in my brain. What served me well in writing comedy suddenly did not serve me with improvisation. You don't get to rewrite. It's one shot and done!

For the first two years of improvisation, my head hurt. I sucked. I am both a feeler and a thinker. And, it was mind-numbingly tough to assimilate all these "rules" and not over-think things on stage.

Source: Keepingithuman.com (a fun shot for my one-woman show, 2015)

You know when you are watching a well-choreographed dancing line and then the camera pans down the line and there's one dancer just dancing to a completely different rhythm? That was (some days still is) me. Today, I embrace dancing to *my* rhythm because it is the source of my creativity and playfulness. It's what makes me *me*.

Learning the process and tenets of improv gets easier, better, and more fun. I am stubborn, and I did not quit after those first two years. Why? I knew if I could do stand-up and sketch, I could learn improvisation, and I knew the payoffs would be a more improvisational mindset. Boy, am I glad I didn't quit! Twelve years after starting improv (on top of stand-up and sketch for eight years before that), I have a blast onstage. It's second nature to me, and I am still evolving and learning. I have earned my 10,000 hours, and then some. No one ever stops growing.

Source: Kathy Klotz-Guest (I am second from right, bottom row)

I knew that improvisation would further hone my funny bone. It did. But what it did for my creativity and risk-taking muscles was the real payday. Improvisation will make you more creative, accepting, fully present with others, and willing to take risks. Improv is not a panacea, but it will lessen your fear of risk. You will embrace experimentation and learn quickly and easily from things that didn't work out so you can get to the things that do. And *that* is an important mindset for marketing and business - especially if you are an entrepreneur.

Source: Kathy Klotz-Guest

With my fellow funny people from my improv group, Make Your Own Damn Sandwich. I am first on left. Collectively, we studied improv comedy at places including ComedySportz, Upright Citizens Brigade (UCB), Second City Hollywood, Annoyance Theater, and BATS to name a few great institutions.

All Business is Personal

I spent years in high-tech marketing, creating products, campaigns and stories and managing teams before I founded my company, *Keeping it Human* ᴸᴹ. Now being human is my philosophy for approaching life, not just marketing. I left high-tech to create a company that valued bringing the personal and human into business. If I hated all that jargon and sterile marketing, I couldn't be alone. I had a jargon-monoxide attack from all the fumes. Seriously, my company could have packaged up all that crap and sold it to the CIA for their enhanced interrogation techniques because that stuff was torture to read and to create. Along the way, I learned that when I shared my story with honesty and humor, others felt the same way. Marketing can be honest, human and fun and get big results. And while I was in corporate marketing, I continued studying and performing comedy – trying, failing, learning and growing.

Today, I perform and write on a weekly basis. It keeps me sharp and creative. Hell, it's also a lot of fun and it's my oxygen (other than actual oxygen!).

Years ago, I also began to wonder how these two worlds in which I live—the business and comedy stages—could assimilate in a way that humanizes and elevates business storytelling and content to a place that transcends the transaction and hits us at our emotional core.

I sat down to map out lessons I learned over the years that I use regularly, and distilled them in a way that would be as simple as possible for others to glean. This book sums up those years of experience in a way that I hope is helpful for you. I still hope you take an improvisation or comedy class. Everyone should. It will do wonders for your risk-taking, speaking and creativity muscles. You'll also have fun if you let go of control, and you just might develop friendships with amazing people. I have. And for all these things, I am grateful.

My hope is to spark your creative juices and humanize your storytelling and content for better results. Using exercises and tips in this book consistently will:

- Get you out of your content rut and away from using the same ideas over and over (that's where the big "a-ha's" happen!)
- Give you methods you can revise and revisit when you want to generate consistently fresh ideas
- Make you a more human storyteller and give you story structures you can adapt and use whenever you need
- Unleash your creativity (alone or in teams)

This Book has Two Parts

The **first part** of this book deals with tips from improvisation to make you a better storyteller and humanize your storytelling.

The **second part** provides exercises for coming up with story and content ideas. You can even use these exercises to come up with sales, brand, and product ideas, and improve your sales processes as well as business models. Apply these exercises to almost anything and get results while having fun.

I use the storytelling techniques from the first half of the book and the exercises from the second half in my business. I have tested all of these exercises and tweaked them before writing them down for you.

If you use even a fraction of the tips in this book consistently (and start with the ones that resonate most with you), you will have more ideas than you will ever need. Write all those great ideas down. You may not use them immediately; yet you may decide later to come back to them. I know you're busy. There is so much out there to keep up with, to read, and to do. It's overwhelming. I get it. I am a working mom, and I can't keep up some days! For those who find time at a premium, read and implement one tip and chapter per day, or just one tip per week. You'll be amazed at the difference in your creative output.

Think "What If"

- *What if we change this one thing?*
- *What if I tried this or that?*
- *What if I just played with no investment in an outcome?*
- *What if there was no failure (there is only learning)?*

"What if" is a great way to approach anything new. Try it!

Source: Keepingithuman.com

Do you want to be safe, or do you want to innovate? Playing content safe—boring, sterile and transactional—won't help you or your customer. And improv techniques, you'll discover, aren't as risky as you might think!

Happy innovating!

Source: Keepingithuman.com

1
EVERYTHING GREAT I LEARNED ABOUT MARKETING CAME FROM COMEDY

I believe all great marketing, like improvisation and comedy in general, is storytelling.

At its core, improv is so much more than comedy. Comedy is the sexy part that gets all the attention. I get it. Comedy is fun, and I love doing it. But improv has done so much more for me than just make me funnier.

Source: gratisography.com

Before we dive into the juicy goodness of applying elements of stage improvisation to business storytelling, I want to differentiate between *improvisation* as a set of stage techniques versus the idea of *improvised*. The latter means made up on the spot. And content can be improvised, certainly. While ditching the script can improve your stories in the moment, the focus in this book is about applying improvisation concepts and exercises purposefully to spark more creative ideas and weave powerful stories that make your audience say, "Yes, that's it! They get me and my needs!" While you can improvise stories on the spot, and I do, this book is really a how-to guide best used with practice and intention.

Eight Lessons of Improvisation

Here are **8 big** lessons (and there are more!) I've learned from improvisation that can take your marketing strategy to the next level:

1. Take Risks
Social engagement requires experimentation. In a world of big data science and analytics, marketing is still part art. Improvisation involves taking creative risks.

The more you experiment, the more you discover what works. As with improvisation, the best way to know if something works is to do it.

Risk is a muscle; when you exercise, it grows. To evolve, marketing must take similar risks. Sometimes things won't work. And some will.

2. Go for Emotional Truth
Improv and comedy are about revealing the truth of the human experience. Great content, too, is about the truth. It's about the truth of being human, having a pain point, and needing to solve it. It's about the truth of needing to be entertained, have fun, and connect with others. All human beings respond to truth.

3. "Yes, and" to Co-Create Something Better
Marketing means co-creating. "Yes, and..." is the cornerstone of improvisation. It's the building block for great scenes.

For example, if your on-stage partner calls you "Mom," you are a mom, and you must build onto the reality your partner creates. When we 'deny' an offer (yes, but...), the scene stalls. "Yes, but" someone in a conversation where you are trying to create something together and watch the reaction you get. "Yes, but" them enough times and that person will stop trying. So would you.

Source: gratisography.com

This happens every day at a subconscious level for most of us. You'll notice that "yes, but..." kills creativity. In cultures filled with people who "yes, but" (which really means "no"), very little co-creating happens.

Great marketing involves "yes, and"-ing your audience. Your customer defines your brand in a way that is meaningful for them. As marketers, we shape it, yet positioning is ultimately in the hearts and minds of customers. Brand control is an illusion, really. Great marketers recognize that successful marketing is an act of co-creation with others— employees, customers, and partners. **Adding on to customers' stories and ideas makes your brand better.**

Raise Your 'But' Awareness

Here's an exercise I like to try with teams:

Wear a rubber band around your wrist for one day. Every time a "but" comes out of your mouth in response to someone else's ideas, snap that band. Seriously. Some of us would have very sore wrists. This activity raises your awareness on how much you use the word before you have really even heard an idea in its entirety. Most of us aren't aware of how much we negate the ideas of others. And, even more so, we often negate our own ideas before giving them a chance. That is just as important to be aware of.

An Example

Your colleague or boss wants to add more features to a product. You don't agree. Here is how most of these conversations go:

Susan: "We need to add feature x to the specs."
Javier: "Ok, but we don't have time to review at this point."
Susan: 'But we said we would circle back on it. So we need to revisit it."
Javier: "But it's not a priority…"

The conversation goes nowhere and causes negative feelings! We've all been on the receiving end, and we've unwittingly done it to others.

Substitute "and" for "but"

When we substitute "and" for "but" it does not mean you have to agree to everything. Using "and" means 'I hear you,' and that is an important step in moving conversations forward. This is important in creating new ideas, in sales, and in conversations where driving agreement becomes important.

I get it. Not every idea is a gem. I have the same experience. If someone has a craptastic idea, you are not committing to implement it. You are simply keeping them in an idea-generating mentality. That matters because that's how we get to the good stuff – by not judging and keeping an open mind. So now we use "and" instead of "but":

Susan: "We need to add feature x to the specs."
Javier: "And we can look at that as the next step after this."
Susan: "And let's review it before the next meeting."
Javier: "And that will help set priorities. We may have to shuffle a few things if that one receives a higher priority."
Susan: "Ok. And we can deal with that when we get there."

In this example, "and" means they are moving forward and agreeing to review a feature. It doesn't mean the feature will be added. It doesn't mean Javier is saying "yes, let's do it." Using "and" here simply means the idea will be reviewed and prioritized along with everything else.

This doesn't mean you should never use "but." When you are collaborating on ideas or trying to get agreement to move forward, "but" has a tendency to get in the way. There's a time and place for "but", just not at the possibility end of the idea funnel. Think of it as important later on at the probability stage of the idea funnel when you are whittling ideas down based on viability. Then, "but" can be useful. It's also useful to signal a disruption of the status quo – and I will talk about that in the next chapter.

4. Make Your Partner Look Good

Marketing is always about your customer. In improvisation, your goal is to make your stage partners look good by accepting what they offer (or what they choose). When you focus only on your choices, you compromise the continuity of the story you are creating together. **Great marketing requires empathy,** and you can connect with your customers by considering ways to make them more successful, and delighted. Drop the focus on your methodology, your jargon, and your baggage. Make your customer (or your customers' customers) the hero of the story.

Source: gratisography.com

5. Listen

Marketing requires listening more than talking. One of the hardest things about improvisation is clearing your head so you can listen to your on-stage partner rather than thinking ahead to what you are going to say next. Being present in the moment allows you to **see opportunity and react spontaneously to what is offered**.

When you listen more than you talk, you hear what your customers are saying about their needs and wants. This allows marketers to react in real time to situations as we evolve towards a new era of 'in the moment' marketing. Think: Chewbacca Mom (Kohl's acted quickly to reach out to her) or Oreo's "Lights Out" moments as examples where companies were listening well and were able to react quickly to opportunities.

6. Tell Stories

Marketing, like improvisation,, is all about storytelling. Stories bring laughter, inspiration, and make us memorable. According to Marketing Professor and author Jennifer Aaker at Stanford University, research shows that people remember stories up to 22X more than facts alone[ii].

Too many facts in improvisation (instead of emotional reactions) can kill a scene. A scene is about people, and the most important thing in improvisation is the relationship the players have with each other on stage. The same is true for marketing. Successful marketing connects with our hearts, not just our heads. **Stories make those emotional connections** so we care about the brand.

7. Let Go

Follow the customer's lead. In improvisation, players need to learn when to lead a scene and when to follow someone else's great idea to move the story forward. When the scene naturally coalesces around someone else's idea, it's in the best interest of the scene to rally around it instead of driving the scene your way. In marketing, **you have to know when to let go and follow your customers' lead**. Great marketing involves allowing our customers to shape those stories. Letting our advocates, our enthusiastic customers, take the wheel allows us to learn what they need and how we can make them look good. Improvisers learn to let go because the **outcomes are usually far better when we build something together**.

8. Embrace Imperfection

Improv embraces imperfection because marketing and brands, like people, are imperfect. In improv, there is no failure in the strict sense. You try something. Maybe it does not work as expected, and you move on. Mistakes are celebrated because they help us learn. To be human is to be imperfect. In improv, little moments of imperfection make scenes better. When improvisers break character and laugh, when they get names wrong, when they poke fun at each other on stage—these moments are all gifts that make stories better and audiences crack up. Stories, like people, are not perfect. Imperfections make things fun, human, and real. A great brand is imperfect and should embrace that. Your marketing will be better for it.

Source: gratisography.com

Part of embracing imperfection is crafting a *ditchable playbook*. **Plan, but always be ready to ditch the playbook. Marketing requires adaptability.** Everyday, unforeseen stuff—both good and bad—happens. When stuff stops working, great marketers improvise.

Improvisation isn't just winging it. Improvisation requires preparation, skill, and big values such as trust. Once you know the rules, you can break them. The same is true of marketing. Marketers who prepare and are willing to adapt will be the ones to succeed in a noisy world of rapid change where the rules are changing all the time. Solid brands adapt easily because they are prepared, yet open, to change.

Marketing is a lot like jazz. Its beauty isn't in the predictable notes; its beauty is in the improvisation. So prepare, be open, let go, and adjust.

These eight principles from improvisation make us better marketers. The goal of this book is to dive more deeply into techniques that involve and build on these principles. And I'll explain a few more principles in detail.

Enjoy the ride!

Next Up...

In the next chapter, we will delve into one of my favorite, simple models for storytelling, the *Story Spine*, and I'll illustrate how to add color to your story.

Are you ready?
Let's do this
Ok...the secret handshake comes later.

Source: Keepingithuman.com

2
ONCE UPON A TIME

"Have the courage to not be funny. A joke will be remembered for a while; a great story will never be forgotten."
- Every great improvisation and sketch instructor I had

The Marketing World is Made Up of Stories

I believe that human stories are the amino acids of meaningful business and of edge-of-your-seat stage work.

Every great story has a narrative arc. From the character's challenge and the rising tension to the action's climax, falling tension and resolution, the narrative arc is how we best experience the emotional ride of an engaging story.

As I mentioned in the introduction, a lot of business storytelling lacks the emotional resonance that we see on the theater stage because it is aimed at a purely "rational" buyer – which, like a unicorn, is a mythical creature! The story arc is how we, as an audience, follow stories emotionally, not intellectually. That is where the deeper and more meaningful connection happens.

Source: gratisography.com

Emotional Resonance Relies on Story Arc

Storytelling models are as varied as they are powerful. A few I learned in business, and a few I learned on the improvisation stage. No single model works in every situation. Because improvisation does such a great job at advancing the human story by adding narrative and emotion, I want to share a few of these models with you. I have used them, and they work! I have made a few tweaks for my needs. You can do that, too, as you become more familiar with each model.

These models help create an arc that moves us through the elements of a story in ways that make your stories pop!

The Story Spine

The first model is a 7-step technique developed by Kenn Adams in his work, *How to Improvise a Full-Length Play: The Art of Spontaneous Theater*. My friend, author, improviser, and trainer, Kat Koppett, was the first to call the model, "The Story Spine."

I love that this model combines the *art* of storytelling with a practical approach that can be applied to business. I have written about it many times and have used it with my own modifications. As you get more experienced and comfortable with its pieces, you can adapt this framework to suit your needs.

The "Story Spine" starts with the classic "Once Upon a Time" opening. This approach is a universal opening that we all recognize, and it works because that's how our human brains are wired: *This happened first, then this happened, and so on.*

And that is exactly why I really like this model – it creates a structure that moves through key parts of the story: this is what exists, then this happens next, then something else happens…until, ultimately, something happens (some changing event/product/service/issue) and there is a big change for your customer. It's the 'because of this, then that" part of the spine that advances that narrative by heightening actions and consequences.

While the spine walks us through a mini-arc, we still need to flesh out and add texture to our story, and I will get into that after I present the model.

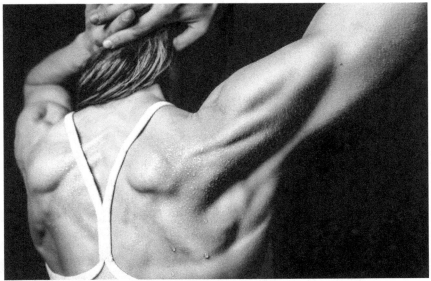

Source: gratisography.com

The 7-Step Story Spine (**my modifications/notes in parentheses**)

Once upon a time…(Opening setting and character established)

Every day…(Establishes the status quo. What is it?)

But, one day… (There is a disruption to the status quo. 'But' makes sense as it signals disruption.)

Because of that…(What happens when things stop working?)

Because of that…(You can repeat this as many times as you need…to get to the "so what" of your story – what's the pain that becomes so great that your character seeks resolution and change?)

Until, finally…(Breakthrough, another change and there is resolution)

And, ever since that day…(Something has changed for your customer (at least for now). What is it and how has it changed their world?)

The story spine is just that – *a spine.* You still have to flesh out specifics for your story to be powerful. You also don't need to use the "Once Upon a Time" wording. It's only there as a guide. When you have all the needed elements, change the wording to something relevant for you. I also talk about this on my podcast[iii] as well as on my blog[iv] and I explain each step if you want more detail.

Things to Focus On with Your "Plot" Arc

Before I get into an example, I want to call attention to the "Every day…" line of the model because it establishes a normal routine. Often times in business, we start our stories with the "fire" — the thick of the conflict when things are broken. There is nothing wrong with doing that. Sometimes starting with "fire" is the most effective narrative choice and it gives our stories variety as compared to always starting at the beginning. Sometimes, however, the magic is in the contrast.

In fact, sometimes starting off with everything working well – in theater, we often refer to it as the beginning of a scene where everything is "happy, healthy, and well," – aids in effective storytelling for two reasons:

1) Too often we go to the place of conflict way too easily. It's an easy fallback. This happens with players on the improvisation stage, too. We anticipate things to break or not work out as promised. However, it's emotionally distressing to always be in "fire mode". People want hope, and they want things to work. Living in constant "fire mode" is emotionally exhausting.

2) The other reason to start off at an established baseline of things working well is so that the disruption to the status quo creates stark contrast. You are telling us how life *used to be* for a character before the turmoil starts. The character in the story is then motivated to alleviate the pain created by disruption. It provides the character with motivating fuel to deal with the challenge at hand. Bookending your stories (beginning and ending) with 'happy, healthy, and well' is a humanizing device that provides optimism and hope for your audience because that is what they want—respite and hope that things won't always be on "fire."

Source: gratisography.com

Elevate your stories by remembering that "happy, healthy, and well" is what people want. Provide those optimistic bookends. Not perfect, just hopeful. People <u>don't need a fairytale ending</u>.[v] They just want to know there is hope that their worlds can be better. Even a failure story is hopeful if it ends on what you learned that could help people.

And it's OK to have some stories start with the fire – just make sure to have variety. You can't have all your stories begin that way. Variety will help your storytelling and allow your audience to feel more connected to the stories you tell.

A Story Spine Example

Once upon a time, Samuel, owner of a private tech company in Silicon Valley, was riding a wave of growth. Things were going well at this stage, and it wasn't too hard to manage his files and data assets while his business was small. He worked a lot to grow his business. Next to his family, it was his passion. He was a self-professed data geek. He kept files in a number of places because he was running hard and fast and believed that redundancy was better than putting all his data eggs in one central basket.

Every day, he updated information in many places because he did not have the data in one secure place to access anywhere in a secure manner. The system worked well up to a point. But as his business grew, his digital file management headache also grew. Eventually, his system of organization became a huge pain that didn't work so well, robbing him of time and resources. He now had to think about security and redundancy of data as well accessibility.

Samuel spent so much time trying to maintain and secure files that he often worked late just to organize things. It was overwhelming, and it added more stress than it helped. Because of that, he missed many family dinners and his son's baseball games. Samuel missed out on home and life balance. And even with all his work, he got behind on things. While he helped his clients use technology, he didn't have time to keep up with his own system needs.

One day, Samuel couldn't find confidential files he needed for a client, and that error cost him business. He couldn't access anything he needed remotely. He tried everything to find a solution until he couldn't take it anymore. Losing that client, the largest prospect he had been interacting with for 3 months, was the last straw. His data system was undermining his business. His home life suffered, too. The stress was too much. And his family was fed up.

Then one day, a friend introduced him to Company X's cloud-based data services. He tried it. Samuel discovered that he could securely access data anywhere, anytime, wherever he was. This was a big deal because he needed security *and* easy, quick access.

Because of this new service, Samuel got more work done quickly, easily and remotely. He didn't have to choose between security and access. And he didn't have try to piecemeal together technology himself.

As a result, he could work wherever he wanted so he could best serve the customer and the business. He closed more business being mobile, and knowing that his – and his customers' data – was secure was a huge relief.

Every day since his friend introduced him to this service, Samuel's organization uses Company X to help not only his business grow; he also entrusts it to serve his customers reliably, too. Now he can focus on what he does best —run his business, have a personal life, and spend quality time with his family, not with his IT department putting out fires.

People Buy Change, Not 'Products' (and Improv is About People and Change)

Company X delivers its service via the cloud; yet, no one needs cloud-based services. Cloud is *how* Company X delivers its services. What matters is that the product allows users to do something (bigger than the product) that they could not do before. In this case, Company X enables information freedom, simplicity, security, and freed-up time. Because Samuel spent so much time trying to organize and find files, he not only lost client files, he missed out on personal family time. So with more time, his personal life is far better. That's Samuel's big personal payoff, not *just* the business benefits.

Your story (in this example I used a typical product / customer story to demonstrate the Story Spine) is always about the people who use what you sell and how their lives are better because of it. Stories have capital *precisely* because they show customers how their lives will be different because of your company. Also, I want to point out that the Story Spine can be used for many types of stories, including brand storytelling. The example above is just one application area for story development.

Improvisation creates human meaning by focusing on relatable people and showing how people change in response to conflict and resolution. Your marketing story should do the same. The above story can still be fleshed out for color. However, you can see how the story spine can help with making sure that a story hits all the core pieces – character, routine, conflict, tension, climax, resolution, and change.

A deep commitment to changing customers' lives for the better—something bigger than any company—is the change your stories must focus on if they are to resonate emotionally with your audience, be memorable, and create compelling calls to action.

Not that long ago, I used my own adaptation of the Story Spine with a technical organization and technical employees. These were scientists that wanted to better explain what they were working on for the benefit of the whole company. The trainer that brought me in said skeptically, "Will technical people get it?" Besides the fact that all human brains (regardless of whether they are technical or not) are wired to make meaning and sense of the world through stories, this model is also about cause and effect. Because of *this*, that happened. We are drawing causal relationships between variables. Isn't that what science does?

So when I used this approach with a group of scientists, one of them, who had been very quiet up to this point, raised his hand excitedly in school like a little kid shouting, "Pick me! Pick me!" When I invited him to share, he proudly stated, "This is the scientific method. This model makes so much sense. We think in stories." He was exactly right. We create stories about problems. And the stories we tell ourselves about the problem determine how we solve those challenges. A hypothesis is an operating story about how something might work. Then we test. Story is the language of science, too.

Source: gratisography.com

I looked over at the once skeptical trainer, and she raised her bottled water to salute me with a large smile. Later she said to me, "You found a way to speak to them in their own language."

"Actually," I said, smiling, "Story is the most fundamental human language. And it's one we all speak. Yes, even scientists."

Frame Your Story

With any model you use, it's important to clearly frame the problem or challenge you are solving. How you frame the story of challenge determines how you solve the challenge.

I like to use a "what comes next" approach to help customers get at the challenge or problem. What has changed in their world? What is the story they tell themselves about this? It's the story that customers tell themselves about their challenge that matters, not what *you* say it is.

Fleshing out Your Basic Story: *What Happens Next?*

In my prior example, you will notice, I added more color to the story than just going through each basic part of the spine, and even more could be added. I like to expand the story spine into human layers with a *because of that* approach. It's a cause and effect thread that gives the plot momentum and leads to the ending, which should be meaningful change.

Using the "What Happens Next," approach moves us through the story until we are able to articulate exactly *how* the customer's situation has changed in human and economic terms.

Use as many *because of that* sentences as you need until you hit on the human heart of your story.

Because of That: An Example

Suppose for this exercise below that the protagonist is a client of yours who buys data security software for a large business. No one exists to buy your stuff. So how can we get to the real human need at the heart of the story?

One way is to apply a series of "because of that" statements to flesh out the real need:

Because of that, employees can access data securely...

Because of that, employees don't have to choose between access and security...

Because of that, employees are able to access data securely from anywhere in the world, including home and on the road...

Because of that, employees are not chained to a desk and now they feel able to do their best work...

Because of that, employees are better able to serve customers' needs at the customers' places of business. They're also better able to work at home when they need to...

Because of that, employees can also use their own smartphones for mobile data and enjoy more work flexibility and freedom, and freedom is a big part of what people need to feel effective...

Because of that, our employees and those of our customers are empowered with

freedom and autonomy to do their best work wherever they are and to do it securely
(Boom – the underlying needs! These are both business and personal benefits.)

Now, if you were writing a story about your enterprise software client and their needs, you could go back and flesh out the story with the above comments about how employees are empowered with freedom, work flexibility, mobility and data security – and then, of course, you have to prove it through a story that demonstrates that. These human elements are the heart of your story.

Emotional Stories Need Color and Commentary

Another really important point about storytelling that I learned in my comedy training was that stories need both color and commentary. What exactly does that mean?

Color adds depth – it's the richness in your story based on character development, setting, and conflict, for example. It is what pulls people into the story initially.

Source: gratisography.com

Commentary is action. We've all watched sports anchors and the great ones give us play-by-play action details. The news is based on action. Commentary advances the narrative and, thus, helps to sustain emotional interest throughout the story arc.

A great story has both commentary (action) and color (depth). The *Story Spine* will help flesh out actions and consequences that engage. The way that you color it with rich details about character, setting, and feelings among other things provides the emotional depth. This book will cover both aspects in upcoming chapters.

Your Turn

Use the *Story Spine* to creative a narrative structure that you flesh out later for your own origin or brand story, your change story, or best customer stories. And you can use elements of this approach with other models. I like to combine approaches, for instance. Try the "What comes next?" series of statements to move through the action and consequences that you want your customers to understand and identify with.

Next Up...

Now you're ready for the next chapter on adding specifics, which is how we add color to heighten emotional resonance.

Source: Keepingithuman.com

3

DELAWARE PUNCH AND STUDEBAKERS

"Every detail is a gift you can use later. Audiences remember specifics."
-*A sketch instructor from Second City*

Details Give Stories Emotional Weight

One of my favorite stage scenes I ever performed was when I was endowed not just as a director; I was specifically endowed as Stanley Kubrick by a fellow improviser. What a huge gift. With that level of specificity, I could make callbacks and puns using titles of Kubrick films (as many as I could remember). And I did.

In this scene, I wore the same thing every day as I went to work in a "Full Metal Jacket," and drank my "Clockwork Orange" for breakfast. My character walked into walls with "Eyes Wide Shut," and I went on a "Space Odyssey" where I met and befriended a "Shining" star and fell in love. The crowd went nuts as they got the references, and because there was an underlying, cohesive story pulling everything together. When you are specific – in this case "Kubrick" vs. "director," you can play with details so much more to the delight of your audience. Specifics have emotional mass that can help alleviate transactional storytelling – which isn't great storytelling at all.

Source: gratisography.com

With specific quirks, eccentricities, and likes and dislikes, a generic protagonist becomes a character people remember. It's the difference between a brilliant, eccentric crime-solving detective and a deeply neurotic, obsessive-compulsive genius widower named "Monk" who drives people nuts and solves crimes like no one else.

And, when you are specific about details, including character, you develop a signature point of view for your story. Every powerful human story with strong characters has a strong point of view because the characters do. So take the time to develop characters using specifics.

I had an improvisation instructor who would stop scenes in practice and ask us to make more specific choices. Whether it's on the improv / comedy stage or the business stage, details create greater emotional resonance —something all business stories need.

To illustrate this point, one improv instructor I knew for years told students a story about a now-famous comedian with whom he once shared the improv stage in Chicago. This particular now-famous improviser made very specific choices that my instructor remembers years later. In one case, this improviser asked for a Delaware Punch, not just a soda. In another instance, another now-famous comic made his vehicle a 1940 Studebaker, not simply a car. That specificity evokes an image of setting, time, and nostalgia in a defined way, and it paints the picture of a person who loves old cars. Now you can play with those details in your story.

In a scene playing video games, imagine saying *Pong* or *Space Invaders* rather than "video game." Now, all of us who remember *Pong* and *Space Invaders* are thinking about all the great memories we have playing the games with our friends. That detail transports us to a different time in our lives. Instead of referring to someone on stage as "my friend," we say "best man at my wedding" or "my roommate at junior high sleep-away camp." Instead of "building" as a setting, it's the "annual employee picnic." A close improviser friend likes to pour drinks in scenes and his characters always enjoy "Hennessey" or "Courvoisier" because Cognac isn't specific enough!

The audience delights in those details because they relate so much more. Specifics paint a very detailed sensory picture that you can easily visualize, smell, and feel. That provides emotional depth. And you can refer back to details later. In improv and in stand-up comedy, we call these later references "call backs." Audiences love them because they can tie a scene together in a way where the pieces just seem to fit.

I was once on a podcast run by a lawyer with a background in improv. I spoke with this host about the power of specificity to create a story for the jury. I gave the following example: Imagine you are working a case that is building towards establishing that one party is unreliable.

To do that, the prosecuting attorney tries to paint a story that not only is this person unreliable in business, he or she is also an absentee parent. That really doesn't tell us much. It gives a headline but not the whole emotional story. Remember, we have to get others to *feel* our story, not just hear it. Now, imagine the prosecuting attorney says, "she missed countless birthdays, sporting events, family gatherings, the kids' milestone graduations...and the kids cried inconsolably at their grandmother's funeral because Mommy wasn't there to comfort them."

All stories hinge on sensory details to fuel emotions. Emotional detail is gripping. Now you know that it's not just that a party was unreliable, you know that they weren't there for key milestones in their kids' lives. Thus, it answers the question "How unreliable?" It leaves more than data; it leaves an emotional imprint. That's what people remember.

What do you want your audiences to feel? Start with that then build details designed to evoke these feelings. That is where adding sensory richness can be a mindful, purposeful exercise with a big payoff.

Adding Sensory Richness

The key is to concentrate on *relevant* details. When you have to get to the point, you can cut out a few details. However, you won't want to skimp on everything.

Below are a few story places where you can weave in sensory details to animate your narrative.

Setting

Where are you? What's the temperature of the immediate environment? Does it add to your stress or to your mood (If it does, it's relevant!)? What's the color of the paint on the walls? If you are in an office, what does it look like? Smell like? What sounds do you hear? Does it put your character at ease or add tension /stress to the story?

Character

What is the point of view of the main character? Who are they? Are they a decision-maker, an employee, a person with a big personality, an impatient, worried person? What is their "lens?" The more you paint character, the more we are pulled into your story.

Source: gratisography.com

What is the main character wearing that might be relevant? What does he look like (style of dress, mannerisms)? What is her facial expression, and how does it change as the story evolves? If that person is making a big decision that weighs on him, how does that fact affect his demeanor, tone, voice, point of view, quirks, beliefs and values, walk, attitude, or external behavior? If it's a founding story of the company, for example, you want to give details about the values of the founders and why they are passionate about creating a movement that makes lives better.   What drives them? What's their deepest belief for a better future for people and why? Characters with distinct points of view are memorable in business storytelling and on the comedy stage.

These details become relevant when we consider the stress of tension and conflict that must be part of the story. People carry stress in their voice, their gait, their speech patterns, their posture, and many other behaviors and expressions.

Conflict / Resolution

What choices must be faced? Are they horrible choices? Uncertain choices? What's at stake for the character if the situation isn't resolved?

How does the character feel about the challenge and the resolution?

How are relief and joy expressed? Show us rather than tell us. Most humans don't announce their feelings all the time. We *show* them. For example, maybe an angry protagonist picks up and then puts objects down in a passive-aggressive way or slams them on a desk. That *shows us* how he or she feels.

Ending

How does the character's expression and body language change? How is he or she feeling at the end of the story? How has their personal and professional world changed?

The Inner World of Feelings

Physical details make stories richer. Another really important way to make stories more memorable is to provide more detail about how the main character is *feeling* throughout the story.

Too much business storytelling is transactional and sterile. We're afraid to talk about feelings. That is weird because we're not robots. Studies show that 92.3% of audiences are, in fact, made of people – with feelings! I don't know about the rest. I've worked for a few of them back in my corporate days. Not fun.

Source: gratisography.com

Instead of talking about how a character in business feels – such as nervous, filled with a sense of risk, scared, vulnerable, worried, happy, excited for opportunity, proud of their work, whatever the emotion – business storytelling often lists things the character did or said. That is not storytelling. That is a transactions list. And it's boring.

Delve a bit into the interiority of your character. Every character has feelings about the situation and challenge at hand. And giving appropriate details creates greater emotional stakes for your audience. Show us how you, your customer, the story's main character, or other characters feel about things throughout the story as situations change. Here are some ways to dive more deeply:

- *How is this person feeling about the situation now? About the challenge ahead?*
- *What's at stake for him/her? How does that make them feel?*
- *How are characters feeling about how things will work out?*
- *How is your main character feeling about the resolution or the end of the story? I hope this would be hopeful about the future! The character might also be feeling trepidatious because that is human. Anxiety mixed with hope is normal and real.*

When characters reveal how they feel, it humanizes the tension and the challenge. Your audience can relate and say, "I get that. I have been there, and I felt that way, too. And yet, I know it's going to be OK."

Even if you don't say it, your audience is thinking, "How will doing business with this company make me look? How will it make me feel?" And if your stories leave people feeling that they are just a transaction to your company, you didn't go deep enough. You want to leave your customer and prospect feeling, "Wow, other customers had those same challenges and felt the way I feel, so maybe there is hope for me."

Source: gratisography.com

When you connect emotionally, your audience feels:

- *This company understands what I am facing.*
- *This company gets the stress I feel if this challenge isn't solved.*
- *This company understands that choosing a vendor reflects on me.*
- *I feel risk in that choice, and I need to feel good about my choices.*
- *I see myself in this company's story and the story of its customers.*
- *I need to feel hope and relief that things can be better.*

Adding Specifics to Our Chapter Two Story

In the last chapter, we applied the "Story Spine" to a story about a tech company owner. Let's revisit that same story and flesh out some details by adding more specificity. And now that we have a basic structure, we can deviate from the original wording a bit:

He got the funding he needed, and, as he walked out of the meeting that got his business launched, Samuel Davis couldn't help but give a big fist-pump. He did it. Yes! Samuel, now owner of a tech company in Silicon Valley, had finally launched his dream company helping businesses better manage technology. He called it "Technical Leg-Up" – a funny name he had thought about way back in college at Marquette University when he knew he wanted to start his business. A transplant from Wisconsin, he loved tech, Green Bay Packers, cheese, and his family – twin boys, aged 10, and his wife. He loved spending time with them playing and coaching football when he wasn't working. And he did love his business. He called himself a "tech nerd" and that was true of most of his customers, too.

An expert at technology himself, even he found it hard to keep up with file management as his business heated up. While it wasn't too hard to manage while his business was small, it got increasingly harder as his business grew, and he didn't have the time to help clients, run the business and work on IT-related issues for his own business. It was too much.

Every day, he updated information in many places because he did not have the data in one secure place to work remotely. But as his business grew, his digital file management headache grew. Eventually, his system of organization became a huge pain that didn't work so well, robbing him of time and resources. He now had to think about security and redundancy of data as well accessibility – that added a whole new layer of risk. He was up to his eyeballs and already stressed about the business and trying to do it all.

It was overwhelming. Because of that, he missed many family dinners and his sons' baseball and football games. Samuel missed out on home and life balance. And his wife, Maria, wasn't too happy, either. And even with all his extra work trying to get caught up, he got behind on things.

Eventually his patchwork system caught up with him and he couldn't find confidential files he needed for a client, and that error cost him business. It was a big account, too. He had been working on this account for months – so this was a big financial hit. He couldn't access anything he needed remotely. Losing that client was the last straw. His data system was undermining his business. That and the stress on his family were too much. Something had to give.

With some trepidation, he tried X. It gave him the ability to securely access data anywhere, anytime, wherever he was and to better manage his data. This was a big deal because he needed security *and* easy, quick access. It also saved him time and a lot of headaches trying to configure a solution on his own.

Over the weeks he used the service, Samuel got more work done quickly and easily, without having to choose between security and access. He closed more business being mobile, going to the customer, and getting out of the office. And, he could spend more time at home not working trying to catch up. That made his home life a lot less stressful.

Today, Samuel continues to rely on X because it helped him grow his business. He was able to scale safely and free up his time to do what does best—run his business and spend quality time with his family, not with his IT department, putting out fires. He's less stressed and so is his family. However, he's got some work to do on his batting average and he owes Maria more date nights. And now he has the time to work on those! (It's OK to use a little humor. You're likely not curing diseases; so your claims should be proportional, specific and realistic. No perfect ending needed. You just need optimism that things can be better.)

A Note About Specificity

It's important to also recognize that in the name of brevity you might not be able to give tons of details. In other words there is a time and place for details. If you are writing long-form content and you have an interesting story (the above was a sales/marketing story...but you might have a really interesting story about an employee who builds homes for Habitat for Humanity in her spare time or an employee who has developed a new product for your company because he had a need and it sparked a bigger innovation), you can take the time to give lots of great details.

If you are giving a live, in-person presentation, you will want to bring your stories to life in front of an audience. If you are in a sales meeting, you likely need to cut some details out. The level of detail is contextual, of course; but in general, establishing the relatability of your character and their challenges is going to be really important to drawing people into your story.

Your Turn

Take one of your stories that you feel is powerful and could really help connect with audiences and add more sensory detail to it. Adapt the level of detail to the situation at hand. Sensory detail makes your story stickier; it acts as an emotional conduit for your story to connect with audiences. You never stop being human in business. Stories should read like it.

Next Up...

In the next chapter, we will explore wants. Just as in improvisation, every business prospect or customer wants something human. And it's *not* your products and services! Articulate that in an emotionally gripping way in your stories in order to connect viscerally and banish boring, transactional stories forever.

Source: Keepingithuman.com

4

EVERYBODY HAS A WANT

"Watching a character try to meet a need creates story. Watching that need get blocked repeatedly, seeing the character get frustrated, and observing how that character still does not give up trying to fill that need creates comedy."
- *Instructor at Second City, Sketch Writing*

It's Always About the Human Want

People don't exist to buy your stuff. They have human needs that are not being met. *That's* why people buy. It really is that simple. Business tends to forget that fundamental point and adds way too much complexity to the process.

When it comes to storytelling, most businesses are stuck at a superficial layer because they come at stories with a "helped a customer make money or save money and/or time" mentality. It's that transactional approach to business that, sadly, permeates way too much organizational storytelling. It's not inspiring or hope-inducing. It's dry, boring, and misses the personal mark.

Sure, the economic "rational benefit," as research calls it, matters. Yet, economics are only *part* of the buyer's consideration process. The bigger part is the *personal* benefit. Think about the story of tech company owner, Samuel, in Chapters Two and Three. His needs were both business and personal, as most buyers' needs are. Stories cannot focus solely on the rational benefit to the exclusion of the personal. Yet, that is what many businesses get wrong.

What's Under the Transaction Hood?

Source: gratisography.com

Peel back the transactional, rational benefits layer and there is a whole other human layer of need. Ask yourself, why is saving or making money important for my buyer? Because human drives such as the need to be successful, appreciated, recognized for competency and credibility, and to achieve financial freedom, among other things, dictate choices.

Speaking to the personal benefit gives marketing the emotional glue it needs to resonate with audiences.

When one client came to me, he was a company founder, a former chef who went to cooking school, who was struggling with his story. He had spent tons of money on building a site, a logo – all of it. Your logo is not your brand, by the way. Your story, however, is. He went to tradeshows for years and had little success. When he approached investors, they asked him, "Why are you building this?" He didn't have that big story nailed down. And because of that, he was headed in a direction that didn't distinguish his site from the competition.

Until this time, the company had been focusing on a tactical need. It had been talking about recipes and thus, it was lost in a sea of competitive sameness. Yet, the founder was insistent that the company was not a recipe site. Recipes are tactical. And why do people want recipes anyway? What does your specific site give them that they really want and need? (Mind you, people can get recipes anywhere). I asked him what his ideal customers really wanted that they could not get other places. He sat in silence for a good while, and then his answer was direct: information. Information translates into freedom to make better choices. That's not about recipes at all. He had done extensive research showing that Millennials were willing to spend more on organic food that was healthier, sustainable, and sourced locally through responsible businesses. The gap was that they didn't always feel like they knew *where* to spend that money and what the best food choices were for their families. That gap represented an opportunity. And this entrepreneur was a dad and chef, so creating healthy food choices for his family was important and he wanted to pass on his knowledge.

With that inspirational and informational nugget in hand, we turned his focus away from recipes and tactical details into a larger mission to make his customers better off by answering the underlying human need at play:

Our big, bold purpose is to inspire people and assist them in making informed choices about real food: food that is fresh, whole, unrefined, unprocessed, and in as natural a state as possible. It's not just about cooking. We believe that living real food means making real and healthy food a way of life.

Technology has increased awareness of the importance of fresh food choices for good health, yet the lack of time and know-how often makes planning and choosing fresh ingredients difficult. Up until now, there has been no convenient, single online resource that simplifies how to make healthy food.

We want to change that by making a difference with today's young adults so they pass this knowledge onto their kids. We want to educate parents so they can teach their children 'living real food' patterns (food buying and preparation) that will help them lead healthier lives.

Our big vision is to empower Millennials — especially millennial moms and dads who are newbies to healthy food — with simple information and tools needed to make eating real food easy and delicious. We also believe that our customers want more than just cooking help for eating healthy; they also want to make a difference in the world with their food choices by supporting sustainable businesses, and by eating fresh, simple, and local. We can help them make more informed choices about the food they buy, prepare and eat.

Quite a big difference between this vision and positioning as a tactical "recipe site," I'd say. Audiences thought so, too. A recipe site with no overarching mission is boring, undifferentiated, and unremarkable. With a focus on information for healthy eating without additives; however, now you can add recipes that bring this story to life. By focusing on a human need for empowerment and healthy living, there is now a credible, connective tissue story that underpins all of the site's content.

The Human Want is Closest to the Sales Dollar

In sales, you must get close to the humanity of your buyer in order to get close to that dollar.

So here's a quick exercise. Answer the following:

People buy from me/my company because

_____

_____

The economic need is

_____

_____

What they really want most is (human need]

_____

_____

We (my company) make peoples' personal lives better by

_____

_____

Can you complete the above statements easily? If so, that is awesome. If not, you'll get there in a few chapters, and then you can refine later.

What Does Your Customer Really Want?

Source: gratisography.com

Every human in every transaction has a want that goes deeper than the transaction itself. In improvisation, each character in a scene—the business equivalent is your prospect or buyer—has a want. Think very simply about your customer: *What do they really want? What do they have to do to get it?*

Understanding this point enables improvisers to create very human characters on stage. Then we move the scene forward by seeing characters try to get what they really want (love, validation, freedom, credibility, visibility, among other things). We also see how they are blocked from satisfying those needs, which creates tension in the story. Then, during the story climax and resolution, we see how / if some of their needs are met. It's never about a transaction. It is about human need fulfillment. All human beings want the same types of things.

So start by understanding the customers' wants and needs at the human level. Ask yourself what's keeping prospects or customers from getting that need met? What are the conflicts and tensions around that? What do they have to deal with constantly that – if you and your company could take away that pain – would give them optimism, relief, and help them do something they couldn't do before? What is the personal pain, not just the professional one? How do you make them and their world better beyond just making money and / or saving money or time?

When your customers want new technology, what they really want is technology that enables them to run their lives and businesses better so they can do other things. They buy technology for hope and optimism that their business and personal lives will be better. Yes, both matter.

It's Abraham Maslow's famous *Hierarchy of Needs* in action.

Hierarchy of Needs

Customers don't make purely rational, logical decisions. No one does. While technology and tools change, people don't. People have human needs for belonging, attachment, peer recognition, stability, risk reduction, visibility, freedom, security, and the list goes on and on! For some audiences, there is also tremendous personal and social value in being the "first to know and use" new technology. Understanding that is important. We're people first, business buyers second.

Source: Kathy Klotz-Guest

Making the Connection Personal

So how do we make storytelling and content work at the emotional level? Making the *emotional connection to personal value* in business is the secret sauce. Research illustrates exactly how important emotional value based on a personal, human need is during purchase consideration in business. And it has to have a rational benefit to even make it that far. That is just table stakes.

Of course, as marketers we already knew this anecdotally, right? In a 2013 study, The Corporate Executive Board (CEB) Marketing Leadership Council, in partnership with Google, found that personal value (for buyers) and social value (perceived by peer group) had twice the effect on commercial purchasing outcomes (purchasing, consideration, advocacy, etc.) as business value, or rational benefit.

In other words, emotional and personal benefits of confidence, peer respect, and career advancement had twice the weight in purchasing decisions as rational benefits such as whether the product could do the technical, functional job it was bought to do (Source: Corporate Executive Board and Google)[vi].

That means emotions trump logic every day of the week when it comes to weighing outcomes. Buying in business always involves personal risk because buyers are people. Your differentiation story (and other stories) *must* take this into account. People also want to be inspired, encouraged – all the things on the Hierarchy of Needs. Content and stories that have a strong emotional component, therefore, are far more effective than just marketing facts alone. Facts are more powerful when wrapped in stories that deliver a powerful emotional punch.

Moreover, research also shows that emotional content is the most shared of all content. More specifically, content that makes people look good and feel good gets shared the most. In fact, campaigns with purely emotional content performed almost twice as well [vii] (31% vs. 16%) as those with only rational content (neurosciencemarketing.com).

All of this underscores the reality that the story you tell about your product and service value – and other stories – must go beyond pure economic and productivity value. No B2B buyer or user makes rational decisions for the good of the organization in a hermetically sealed environment without regard for his or her own personal needs. Every buyer feels the need to mitigate risk for the business and personal risk for himself / herself, and also for the team he or she works for.

It is your job to make your customer look good to his or her organization (a key concept in improv), and that means you need to address how you will reduce your customers' personal risk, in addition to mitigating business risk. When a customer looks good, both the organization and customer win. When things go wrong, your customer takes a personal hit. Marketing should speak to that personal concern in a meaningful way.

The human need then becomes the central part of your story. Just like in improvisation, a great business story ending must focus on how your customer's situation has changed. How are they better off *personally,* not just professionally, because of you. This is why your story must end on a personal triumph, not the economic one, if you want to have impact. Transactions are not only emotionally unsatisfying; they are boring. So end on how your customer is better off personally and you turn story endings from crappy to happy.

For example, consider the marketing VP on your sales list. How will your services make her look good to her boss and enhance her reputation?

How will your IT services mitigate the CIO's professional and personal risk?

Or maybe you sell to small businesses – so will your PR services get them new clients, visibility and the name recognition that they want?

How will your SEO services enable your customers to grow and achieve their vision of autonomy and financial stability?

Even if your clients are consumers, they want something more. If you sell pet supplies, your customers want happy pets. Their pets are deeply loved members of their families, not simply animals they adopted. It's not about buying pet food; it's about buying the best product for the continued health of a 4-legged (in that case) loved one.

That CFO to whom you sell business insurance isn't concerned exclusively with the corporate bottom line. He's also worried about his own bottom line. And if the organization is at risk, so is he personally.

Jan, a woman in her late 50s, cried into the phone as she told me how hard it was for her to let go of her baby, an educational materials content company founded over 25 years ago to help grade-school students with science and math. And she felt she had few options left.

Her company wasn't doing well, and it had been her life's work for the last quarter of a century. "It outlasted my marriage," she managed to laugh through her tears. "I gave it everything I had." For Jan, everything came to a head in 2010. The economy had fallen over a cliff in the wake of the housing crisis. The publishing world had changed, and she battled more competition. Schools, her primary customers, were cutting back on spending because the deep budget cuts were quick, unrelenting, and brutal. Her son did not want to take over the business; he was a big part of the reason she started the company. He had special learning needs and, a teacher herself; she could not find materials she needed for her son or for other kids who had special needs. Soon she discovered it wasn't just kids with learning disabilities who needed special materials; it was most kids because a lot of schools didn't have good supplemental science and math workbook materials.

Jan didn't just need storytelling to sell more products. She needed a differentiated story so that she could attract a buyer or a larger partner with money to spend. Not just any buyer would do.   Jan wanted to attract a buyer that would take care of her baby in a way she couldn't. The only other alternative was to shut the company down. And that, she said, felt like "pulling the plug." It was all too much to think about, and the decision was causing her tremendous emotional distress.

She said how embarrassed she was to lose it on the phone with someone whom she had just met – virtually (we had not met in person at this point). I had never had a prospect cry before. At first, I didn't know what to do. I felt like I was witnessing grief, and I was. I felt her deep pain and conflict. In that exact moment of listening without thinking or saying anything, the personal issue was so real and raw. It hit me hard. She was grieving a transition because her business is her baby. Had I only talked about money and selling for the greatest amount, I would have missed the biggest need for her—to find a home for her *baby*. As a business owner, I understood. We put everything into our businesses. Businesses are an extension of you and everything you love and believe in. This was more than a business; for her, it was a *mission*.

Source: gratisography.com

I told her, "I understand this is your baby. You have nurtured it for over 25 years. It is your life's work. This isn't just about money. This is about making sure your baby thrives in the hands of an investor that will grow it, nurture it, and treat it with care—the way that you would have if you could. So we're going to create some storytelling around possibilities for growth. The goal is to make sure your story attracts buyers who share your vision for taking care of your kid. Your baby is up for adoption and we are going to find it a loving home."

She fell silent for a few seconds. It seemed an eternity because the tension was so palpable and she had the courage to be so vulnerable with me. I was in awe. If this were a different situation, I would appropriately lighten things up with some levity that my clients usually love. I felt the weight of her worry and I didn't want to diminish that. (This is where sometimes as mentioned in long-form improvisation you play the scenes with real emotion).

She finally blew her nose into the phone (it was loud!) then said to me, "You are the first person that I have talked with that understands the personal journey this has been for me. This is my life's work."

I helped her shape a story of new beginnings, of commitment to education and to change as the publishing industry is changing. A larger company who believed in her story of the future soon bought her small firm. The acquiring company was willing to invest in it rather than buy it solely for the name and clients. She received enough money to retire, but instead, she took a job as SVP at the new company in order to help shape its next chapter. For her, the personal need was to see her legacy thrive and that was more important than the economic need of finding a buyer at the highest price.

Add Emotional Resonance to Increase Personal Value

To increase emotional resonance (and emotionally engaging content is anything but boring), and the perception of personal value, be sure that your stories answer many of the following questions:

- How do you make customers' personal lives better, easier, simpler?

- What can customers do because of your offerings that they couldn't do before?

- How does your product improve buyers' emotional and professional well-being?

- How does your product or service enhance buyers' reputations /

visibility, and/or reduce personal risk?

- How does your product or service create social/peer value of respect, credibility, and career enhancement?

About a year ago I attended a few marketing team strategy discussions for a client because the VP thought I could help identify some challenges. This company offered a hosted budgeting and forecasting solution and positioned itself as a better alternative to Excel, its largest competition. The company claimed that it could lower closing costs for accounting each month (it never said how much) and that it could reduce errors in Excel. I asked how big the problem errors in Excel were for their target audience. They said it wasn't as big an issue in the minds of the customers. An issue to be sure, but a small one that did not motivate many prospects enough to switch to a new provider quickly and easily.

And many of the users didn't see the status quo as unsustainable. In direct colloquial language, Excel "ain't broken!"

So what problem, then, is your solution really solving for buyers? They don't know they're 'supposed' to have an Excel problem. To the buyer, your solution doesn't address a problem they have. In short, their story focused on the wrong challenge.

Here is a big a-ha from the research: many organizations spend three weeks closing out the books each month. That means an accounting team spends 75% of its time looking backwards rather than being forward-looking about where the company could better invest its time and money. Time is more of an issue than Excel not working. What could CFOs and their accounting organizations do if they could cut the amount of time spent closing books in half or more?

Time is the key asset being wasted here. And one big story stood out from the research: a CFO who used that extra time to refocus her team on thinking about where they could invest money and resources more wisely. She had team members review contracts, make suggestions, and look for ways to save and make money. In one case, her team member was able to review and renegotiate a contract with old terms to save the company $5MM, all because the company saved time and could now be forward-looking. This is about a lot more than the transaction of time and money here, although that matters, yes. That CFO and her team became heroes to her organization. That meant being viewed internally not as "bean counters" but, rather, as forward-thinking strategists. With that, the CFO could justify adding to her team.

Selling a solution for Excel when it's not broken is transactional and it misses the human layer, as well as the real problem. Selling time and what you could do with two extra weeks a month became a more successful campaign-focus for the company. Campaigns telling that story in both long and short-form got more people to take action. Simply put, the stories focusing on time and making teams look good spoke to decision makers' business and human needs to be viewed more strategically within their organizations.

Increasing Emotion with Comic Heightening

As the opening quote of this chapter states, comedy comes from seeing characters get blocked as they pursue their wants, and yet they are still compelled to do so. They can't help it! Sometimes you may want to heighten the comic tension in your story. A great way to do that effectively, therefore, is to show how the character is prevented from getting what he or she wants and how that character is still driven to keep chasing those wants! When people get blocked and still pursue their human needs in strange ways, audiences can't help but laugh. The blocks, of course, should be benign; meaning no one gets hurt. Benign blocks are funny. Serious blocks create serious drama. That's different.

Source: gratisography.com

One of my all-time favorite scenes I ever did came at a theater years ago when I did a two-person scene pretending to be partners. In this scene, my fellow improviser, Jane, and I just had a great time cracking each other up.

Early in the scene, we had been endowed with an audience suggestion of "cat." We were a couple, and we used cats, our pets, as a way to relate to each other. Cats became the focus for our dysfunctional communication. In the scene, I was holding the cat when she, my partner, came home late without calling. She came into the scene that I established through object work (miming objects) was our kitchen, picked up one of our many cats with her "object work" (pretending to stroke a cat), and announced her hard day.

I responded, stroking a pretend cat in my arms. "Well, this cat would have appreciated if your cat would have called to let us know you would be late."

Without expressly saying it, I communicated to my scene partner that this was a "game." We had found the game in the scene, which in this context is the recurring joke that allowed us to exaggerate and heighten things to a comically wonderful place.

My scene partner picked up on my subtle signal and responded, pretending to hold a cat, "Well, if your cat would find some outside hobbies, and not be so worried about what this cat does, that would be great."

The audience quickly perceived the game and cracked up. Pets became the metaphor and conduit for our relationship. We spoke how we felt about our relationship through our pets. And we didn't need to say that. Our choices made that crystal clear. From there, we just kept heightening:

> "Well, Mr. Pickles here thinks we don't connect enough."
> "And Fluffy, here, thinks we need a weekend in Vermont to clear the air."
> "Well Mr. Pickles needs space in the relationship…Fluffy can certainly understand that, right?"
> "Fluffy doesn't understand why Mr. Pickles is so callous and rude about it!"

It got increasingly funny very quickly.

So if you want to weave humorous tension into your story – and this can make your story more entertaining – show how your characters are prevented from getting what they want (in this case above, one person wants freedom, and the other wants closeness and better communication) and yet still try to get what they want, and then show how things escalate from there. Then, when you are ready to reduce that tension, you can introduce the resolution to the challenge – meaning, you can give the characters what they want. Again, we want to see change and optimism.

Even in a business story, you can have levity. This is how funny content and stories can be created. People will see themselves in your protagonist who is getting blocked (the manager who has to deal with everyone speaking in jargon and gets increasingly frustrated, the small business that is tired of people negotiating services for free, the data analyst that is trying to make marketing recommendations only to discover that the data from listening tools keeps changing every minute, and she has to start over again!).

Your audience will laugh if you show their pain points because they recognize the struggle ("that happens to me all the time!") and that is a great release of tension. As long as you move on with the resolution and show optimism, yes, you can comically heighten even (especially – it needs it!) in business. Ultimately, you still have to have that story connect in some way to their emotional needs in order for it to be effective.

Tips Checklist

✓ Does your storytelling clearly identify a human need? If not, figure out which need is primary.
✓ Is it clear what is at stake for your character if that big need isn't met?
✓ What happens when your customer is blocked from getting what they need and want?
✓ How does your story show that your customer is better off both professionally and personally because of you?

Next Up...

Always remember the big human need at the center of your story. In the next chapter, we'll dive a bit deeper into creating a human drama. *All* storytelling is a about human drama.

You got this! Let's boogie to the next chapter.

Source: Keepingithuman.com

5
IT'S ABOUT US

"A great story has a 'we.' Relationships are emotional glue."
- Improv instructor I had for many years

Before I go further on applying improvisation principles to business storytelling (and in this chapter, we discuss the power of relationships), I want to cover the key elements of all great storytelling.

Source: Kathy Klotz-Guest

Remarkable Stories Need Five Elements (Kathy's List)

This is *my* list as I've told stories over the years and have boiled down all the approaches into the simplest process for me and for my clients. Other storytellers will have their lists, although I am sure we will agree on many, though likely not all, of these elements:

1. Protagonist **and setting**– Your main character (and the setting he or she finds himself/herself in). Who is this person, and what does he or she want? The main character is the focus for all the action. What is at stake for her or him in your story? Give us some idea of the setting the protagonist is in. Long-form stories will require more details. For example, a standout customer success story will have these. If you are giving a presentation, you will want details to enrich your telling of the story because you are informing and entertaining. If you are in sales meeting with a prospect, you can leave some of these details out (though not all) because information rather than entertainment is your focus. It is all about context. Even so, establishing a human element to make people care matters. And even when information is your primary objective, you don't have to be boring! Boring is not a necessity; it's a choice.

2. Challenge – The issue at hand. What happens if the person does not solve the challenge? Why does this challenge matter and what is the urgency? Why must it be solved? Make sure the emotional and professional stakes are clear when you describe it.

3. Tension and conflict –Every great story has conflict. Without a challenge, the protagonist will not pass through a narrative arc that results in meaningful change. Conflict should build to a key inflection point (a big decision / action moment). Inflection points add emotionally charged tension to be released later. Comedy and exaggeration can be used to heighten tension.

4. Resolution – It doesn't have to be a perfect ending. Real is better than "tidy." While your audience does want to see resolution, it doesn't have to be a fairytale ending. Believable is relatable.

5. Change and ending– How is the main character changed? How will your protagonist's life be better? And this change can also include others. If it's a founding story, for example, how will future customers be better off in a way that was not available before because of this new company? How are the founders changed because of the company? Change is part of a gripping story. And the more powerful the conflict, the more change there is. Conflict changes us as human beings. This is not about transactional (economic) change. It is about personal, human change. How is this person's world better, and how is the world itself better (not perfect, just better)? Think 'hope and optimism.'

While all of the above are important for great storytelling, the three C's below are areas to highlight because these, more than the other elements, frequently get shortchanged in business storytelling in my experience:

Character
Challenge / Climax
Change

Make sure these areas are fleshed out. Your stories will be better for it. We will touch on all of these in this chapter and the next one.

Source: Kathy Klotz-Guest / Keepingithuman.com

Great Storytelling Needs a Human Frame

Too often, I see companies create impersonal narratives using entities as protagonists. I've said this before and it bears repeating because it's that important (and I am a mom so I'm going to repeat this! Ha!):

Companies, faceless teams, and organizations can't be the main characters in your business story. They don't have human relationships and feelings and, consequently, they make crappy protagonists.

Source: gratisography.com

You can't build powerful relationships in your stories unless you anchor your story through the lens of a specific person or people. If you are telling an origin story, anchor it through the lens of the founders. If you are telling a customer story, it's not the corporation you serve but the buyer and/or user, or team director for example, who is closest to your service and is most affected by the purchase. If you want to tell a story about company values, tell it through the lens of a specific employee or a specific team. People relate to stories about people. And only people have relationships. "The company did this and that" is a crappy transaction report, not a story.

About four years ago, I was asked to help an executive at a large tech company shape a presentation he would be giving for a large internal sales force and some external partners, including resellers. In the VP's conversation with me about how important people were to the company, he often used phrases like, "It's all about people." Yet, in the actual presentation he gave me to review, all he talked about was the company and the technology. He didn't mention people once. So I stopped him and said, "You told me people are important to your company. Yet, in your presentation, you talk only about technology. You don't even mention people, let alone specific examples. You can't have a great story without talking about people. That means your whole mantra of 'it's about people' isn't credible."

This was hard to say because he had put in a lot of time preparing. I also knew there was a better, more powerful story waiting to be told here and I needed to be direct so we could change course quickly. There was no mention of people, no passion about the team, and no narrative arc in a presentation he was going to give to about 1,000 sales*people*. Why would salespeople get excited over this?

He shook his head and said, "I hadn't even thought about that in all the time I spent preparing. How could I not see it?"

"We all have blind spots, including me, " I said. "Now we have to get to work because there is a great story to excavate!"

Together, (after I threw out those slides!) we reshaped a powerful story about how a specific team at his company used technology to help local government workers get up and running after disasters. Instead of focusing on technology, we focused his presentation through the lens of one particularly potent example using people.

A team of dedicated service and engineering employees at that company, initially led by John and Ashok, had found a way to bring technology into areas affected by the damaging floods in Queensland, Australia in 2011. This team didn't sleep for days. Instead, they acquired boats and trucks of servers and equipment and figured out how to deploy them to flooded areas, and they worked to restore servers so businesses and governments could be fully operational as soon as possible. They worked closely with government teams who needed the technology and technical know-how to coordinate rescue efforts. This small group of customer-focused technical people got into affected areas, figured out how to set up servers and communications stations, and worked round the clock to aid rescue teams in whatever ways they could. Without these systems, time-critical rescue efforts were stymied.

The heart of this story wasn't about technology, though it played a role, certainly. Innovative teams of people came up with ways to help other people in times of disaster. It was people helping people, their customers, and even people who weren't their customers (yet!), in the midst of really difficult circumstances. They accomplished this through the hard work of dedicated teams who found ingenious ways to get technology into areas so rescue teams could connect, collaborate, save lives, and rebuild. They got local government operations working again by restoring technology. Then, this company's teams along with dedicated reseller teams got local businesses up and running. It fanned out from there until towns were getting back on their feet and using technology to help do that. *That* was this company's best story. Especially because dedicated service is part of the company's differentiation and that does not happen without amazing people who go the extra mile in order to be of service. That is a story salespeople can get excited about, champion and retell!

As a consequence of these events, this company was then asked to co-create (with the country's disaster response agency) a prototype of an emergency vehicle, fully equipped with servers, routers, and Internet equipment to be deployed in future emergency situations.

The only reason technology exists in the first place is to make things better and easier for *people*. That is what a great story highlights: human stakes, human interactions, and human change for the better.

Anchoring your business story through a human lens is imperative for building that visceral connection with your audience. That is why stories about relationships trump transactional stories every day of the week! Boom (obligatory mic-drop)!

Source: Robert Bejil by CC 2.0[viii]

Create Strong Characters with a Clear Want

Great stories pull us in by making us care about characters and the relationships at stake.

Your characters can be ordinary people doing extraordinary things in their business or can be about people doing ordinary things extraordinarily – going above and beyond – as exhibited in the above company story about its employees and the flooding in Australia. Or, maybe they are just ordinary people with ordinary needs who change things in some small way. Simple stories told well are sexy.

Maybe the main character in your story is your business partner if you sell largely through channels. How is your big partner using your services to make others look good? Anchor that story through your main contact, buyer, user, or feature members of that team. You can cast a wonderful spotlight on your corporate partner through human interviews focusing on particular people closest to the work.

The same is true of telling your company's values through employee stories. A few years ago one of my favorite stories online was about a specific UPS driver (and the story was featured on the UPS Facebook page) who would take care of stray dogs on his route. And one particular dog was malnourished and he took care of this dog and nurtured it back to health. The story had nothing to do with UPS services; yet, it had everything to do with the organization's values around community. The drivers are members of the communities they work in. Don't talk about organizational values by talking about the organization; show those values at work through stories about specific employees and the differences they make in their neighborhoods.

A strong character gives your audience a huge emotional investment in the outcome. You can worry a lot less about plot and having a "fancy story" when you focus on character development. Simple stories with characters that are human, real, and relatable, work well. And you can see the difference in how that facilitates relationships in the story and with your audience.

A Tale of Two Stories

It was the best of stories. It was the worst of stories. Yes, I couldn't resist. Imagine the following two stories:

Business Story One

A business owner has lost her customer data. She is incredibly upset. She calls her outsourced IT department. That company works to restore the business owner's data. The data is retrieved from a backup. The business owner gets her data back and is happy.

Not a great story. However, it's what you expect. It's what I call "table stakes." It does the job superficially, yet not emotionally. It's a transaction – it's literally a list of what happened without emotional context. I can't identify with either the customer or the provider at any level of depth because they are faceless entities.

Business Story Two

Lori scrimped and saved to open her bakery business featuring recipes from both of her grandmothers. The business is a dream she had wanted since college. After fifteen years in corporate America, she found the courage, cash, and resources to open her store. Her husband and kids would help by working in the store on weekends, and Lori would hold neighborhood events at the bakery for kids, pets, and families, including pet adoption days, networking events for singles, and fundraisers for local non-profits. The bakery even sponsored a local baseball team her daughter played on. The business was a lively neighborhood hub of connection and family for Lori's community.

One day, due to computer issues, she lost all her customer data, including her loyalty program information. Lori had a backup, but it wasn't working. She feared she had been hacked. She was beside her self with worry about how she would recover that information. More than that, she worried about how customers would trust her with their data if personal information (such as emails) was compromised. Worse, if she has to ask people to resubmit information, it would alert her customers that something was wrong and they might think she was not a competent business owner. Lori cared about her business and she cared a lot about her customers' personal information. Their trust in her meant so much.

In a panic, she called her partner, Speedy IT (fictitious name), but it was 6 p.m. Robert answered. By the next morning, the company had recovered all her information. Led by her dedicated contact, Robert, the team had worked all night. With donuts in hand, Robert arrived at 6:30 a.m. the next morning to her shop with a new backup system. He showed her how to operate it and create a duplicate copy offsite. Lori felt a weight lifted off her shoulders. She was so happy that she held a small business event at her bakery to help educate her many business friends about securing their data and eliminating those data nightmares, all with the help of Robert and his team.

Which story resonates with you?

Probably number two because you are a human being! The first story is transactional. The second story focuses on a human drama, on a relationship between Lori and her bakery, on Lori's relationship with her customers and community (and we see how important they are to her), and between Lori and her IT company, specifically with her contact Robert, who takes service to whole new levels. Because of that detail, we better understand the emotional stakes in this story. There is a lot at stake for Lori personally and professionally. And that is the point. We could even expand this story further by talking to her employees and doing an update on Lori's business (a great way to do serial storytelling) and all the good her business does for the community, including sponsoring kids' sports teams. Then, the focus is on Lori and, by the way, we help her with her technology needs. Now I care about Lori and I can see that both the customer and client companies care about their customers. And if I am Speedy IT telling this story, I want audiences to know that my company's teams care about customers and that they can expect this kind of dedicated service when they work with "our company." This story leaves a bigger emotional footprint than a transactional story could.

Relationships on the Improv Stage

Here's another way to look at the issue of transaction versus focusing on human relationships, and the difference it makes in your stories.

Imagine a play opens with the following scene: Two friends are bowling at the lanes they frequent. They discuss the mechanics of bowling, their scores, bowling techniques, and getting bowler's "tendonitis," among other things related to bowling.

Source: Kathy Klotz-Guest

Not super exciting, right? It quickly becomes a boring scene with no human need, no deeper connection. It's just a superficial conversation about bowling. Sure, we might get a few laughs, if we're lucky. Yet, you are in trouble if your audience doesn't care about bowling. And, most people won't care. Bowling has nothing to do with relationships between the people on stage.

Now, imagine these same two friends, while bowling, are talking about their spouses and kids and about their relationship as friends. They discuss not being able to connect with each other anymore because life gets in the way, and they feel they've lost some of their mojo as middle-aged men. They want to rekindle their friendship and do more fun guy stuff together so they can feel alive and young again! The conversation transitions to their respective businesses. One friend worries aloud about having enough business insurance. He feels vulnerable because his concerns involve his family and reputation. The other friend, who happens to sell business insurance, talks to the first about protecting his assets, his business, and his family.

Which scene would you rather watch? I am guessing number two. By the time we get to the business lens of the scene in the second story, we know who these two friends are to each other, what's important to them, and what relationships they value. The transaction is never the focus.

Storytelling Relationships - From the 'Me' to 'We'

Great stories in business and on the stage involve solid relationships. Consider the characters in a story and how fleshing out their relationships to others and adding specific details (chapter three) in the story can provide emotional richness:

The CFO of a private equity firm for 20 years. What is her relationship to the company, to her job, to her employees? How does she navigate the company to success during difficult times? What is the relationship to the audience and their needs?

A "mompreneur" of an app company that is self-funded. Who is she, and what drives her? What is she passionate about? What is her relationship to the company and to the challenge she is solving? Likely it's a personal issue that she is solving because of something in her own experience. That's critical to understanding if it drives the passion she has for business (all business is personal!).

For example, if she created a special blanket for premature babies to help with their warmth and body temperatures because her child was born prematurely, that revelation becomes a key part of her big "why" story. Why should the audience care? Every powerful origin and mission story moves from me (the founder or founders) to the "we" and us of your audience – so that the audience sees themselves in this story.

Here are a few relationships you can explore to deepen the human element in your stories:

- What is the relationship of the main character to the company he or she works for? (founder, customer, employee?) What's unique about it, if anything?
- What's the relationship of a founder or executive to the people who work for him or her?
- What's the relationship of an employee you are highlighting to the community he or she lives in and how does this person make a difference?
- How do teams work well together (explore a particular team through the lens of specific members and how they relate to each other or maybe to customers and how they innovate together)?
- What's the relationship of a partner to the vendor?
- What's the relationship of the employee to a company's mission or values (beyond just the job)?
- If it's a customer story, what is the relationship of the buyer/main character with the provider (be sure to use a human lens here)?
- What is the relationship of the protagonist to the conflict? Why does it matter?
- What is the relationship of characters in the story to each other (maybe the story is about a team leader and her team or about a business owner and his customers)?

Emotional Reactions and Empathy

Another important part to creating heightened human drama and relationships in storytelling is big and honest emotional reactions. People react to stress, conflict, happiness and joy in different ways, but all people have emotional reactions.

Source: gratisography.com

Big emotional reactions are the glue that binds two or more characters on an improv stage as they explore relationships.

People exhibit emotions as they experience them. So this idea of not going there because "it's business," is bullshit. I said it! When we feel risk, insecurity, fear, uncertainty, betrayal, or overwhelm, happiness, joy, excitement, love, surprise, or whatever big emotion, we react accordingly. Imagine seeing a play where people didn't react to either great or devastating news. You would think there was something wrong with them. It's weird and boring.

So another way to humanize your storytelling is to embrace and demonstrate emotional human reactions where appropriate. You don't have to go way over the top, but when shit happens in business, people react. I do, you do, and we all do. "Playing it real" as we talk about in long-form improvisation heightens the audience's authentic connection to your story.

Empathy in
Storytelling
is like the
Hokey Pokey
- it *IS* what
it's all about.

Kathy Klotz-Guest

#kathyklotzguest / #keepingithuman

Source: Keepingithuman.com

Suppose I told you a story about a startup where the founder laid off people in a very cold and emotionally distant way. You would glean that the founder didn't really care about the people he was letting go. The story is delivered in a cold, 'matter of fact' way and that makes people angry. They would rightly think *what a jerk*. That may not actually be true, yet without emotional reactions in the story, we would not have that contextual information. All the information we have is void of feeling. Based on that, it seems like a robot is running the company.

Now here is another version with specifics including emotional reactions and a relationship with his employees:

Ivan got off the phone, wiped the profuse sweat off his face, and put his hands on his head. He took a minute to collect himself, sighed, and looked longingly out the window, shaking his head. He finally looked up at his admin, Angela, fighting back tears welling up in his eyes, and said, "We did not get the funding we need to make payroll for all employees. I built this company. Those people are my family. Now, through no fault of theirs, I am in the horrible situation of laying off members of my family."

Your reaction to the two stories as the audience is drastically different, I suspect. In the second case, you see a big, human side. Now, we have brought empathy to both the founder *and* his employees. That's a powerful difference.

Having empathy for your audience allows us, as storytellers, to create connections with our audience. Just as on a stage, relationships, human framing, and big emotional reactions will serve you well in your business stories because they will help you demonstrate greater empathy. Or my name isn't Bob! Well, because it isn't. But my point stands. Side note: as a kid I declared a new name every week. I didn't like my first name. So, you know, there was *no acting* in my house whatsoever that would ever indicate that I would be a storyteller, comic, and improviser as an adult!

Tips Checklist

Always anchor your story through a human lens. Use a partner, an employee, or a customer as your human frame. We don't empathize with or trust companies. Mostly, we just want to slap them! Make your human anchor credible and relatable:

- ✓ Develop characters so we are drawn in. Who are they? What do they want? Everyone has a deeper emotional want.
- ✓ Tell us what is at stake for that character if the need is not met.
- ✓ What is the relationship of that character to the company? To the challenge at hand? Why should we care?
- ✓ Explore relationships that are relevant to a compelling human drama. Relationships establish a "we" bond with the audience.
- ✓ Show real human reactions in your story where needed.
- ✓ Create empathy for your protagonist and all your characters where appropriate. This shows empathy for your audience.

Next Up...

Now you have ideas to help highlight human drama in your business stories – with a human framing, with the exploration of relationships, and big reactions. With that, your stories will be anything but boring! In the next chapter, we'll cover conflict and change—two more important parts to any compelling story—on the improvisation *and* business stages!

Source: Keepingithuman.com

6
SPARE SOME CONFLICT AND CHANGE?

"Conflict creates the catalyst for change, and we want to see characters be changed."
-*Improv instructor in SF Bay Area*

In improv, players can start out scenes happy, healthy, and well. Then, disruption happens. At the end of the scene, players come together again. This doesn't always happen. However, it's a powerful storytelling approach.

Thus, the short arc of a scene on the improvisation stage can be: *Togetherness -> Disruption -> Resolution (togetherness in a new way)*

What does this simple axiom mean? It does not mean that endings are perfect. It *does* mean that people are changed by what has happened. Challenges change people. Audiences want to see characters changed by what has happened. This is true of all storytelling, even in business.

Recall the 7-step "Story Spine" in the early part of this book. You'll remember that characters establish a routine ("Once Upon a Time…And Every Day…."), then a disruption happens ("Until (or But) One Day…"), and that disruption is a change in the status quo. Something breaks or stops working, and conflict is introduced. The main character or characters cannot continue as if nothing has happened. Ultimately, things must change and characters must change, too, in order to end up at a new "normal" in how they relate to each other and to the new reality of the situation. And with change comes powerful opportunity.

Change is Essential in Meaningful Storytelling

In all storytelling, audiences want to see characters change. In improvisation, that arc sometimes includes status shifts where high and low-status character switch places. Sometimes we see role reversals. Imagine a husband and wife or a mom and her children swapping roles. Sometimes we see both – imagine a janitor and a CEO switch roles (this is both a status shift and a role-reversal).

Audiences crave change because it is emotionally satisfying, and we desire change in our own lives. Transaction scenes don't work in improvisation for the same reasons they suck in business narratives: it's unsatisfying. Where is the change and optimism at the personal level?

I believe that you cannot have a meaningful story without change in your character's world, no matter how small it is. Some marketers use the word story to mean a lot of things that I would not consider true "storytelling" in the purest sense of the word. "Story" has lost a bit of its potency in being bandied about so much. As I explained, a compelling story (as I define it) must have a clear protagonist, challenge, tension, resolution, and end with change.

That means one or more characters must demonstrate that they have been personally changed by the relationship, the challenge, and the circumstances.

Without Conflict, There is No Change

Source: gratisography.com

Far too often, businesses want to talk only about the challenges their customers face. Sometimes, even then, they downplay the degree of obstacles. Businesses are reluctant to talk about their own challenges, missteps, and failures because they erroneously think that to do is "so negative."

Yet, all effective stories must have tension, conflict, and challenge because we identify with conflict. As Kendall Haven, a storytelling researcher, has explained from his findings on what happens in the brain when we hear stories: audiences look for conflict as soon as they hear the beginning of a story. We think *how is the protagonist going to solve that issue? I have the same or similar conflict.* I believe that without conflict, there is no change (and no story in the classic sense).

A trigger event is pivotal because it is where the status quo unravels and the challenge is introduced. Mythologist and author of *Hero of a Thousand Faces* who first described the stages of the universal "Hero's Journey" story, Joseph Campbell, calls the trigger the "inciting incident." And it matters because it ushers in events that lead to change. And stories are about some level of transformation – even if the change is small. This is a really important point worth reiterating – your conflict and change don't have to be huge or earth-shattering to be meaningful. Small changes, for example a mindset change, can be incredibly powerful because it is the precursor for a character to act differently in order to transform his or her life.

Source: gratisography.com

Managing conflict is how we improve, change, and grow. However, just as with the stage, we don't have to jump right into conflict. It's OK to establish the character first and make us care.

End with Hope, Not Perfection

The key question *your business audience* will ask is *how are characters changed positively by the conflict?*

Source: Kathy Klotz-Guest Graphic design credit: Christopher Rizzo

On the business stage and page, your prospects want to know how your customers, partners and employees' lives are better off because of your company, its values, and its products and services, no matter how small the change.

If your business story involves the CEO of a company staring down a downsizing situation, how will laying off people change him or her personally? How can that kind of human loss make him and the company better and more compassionate as a result?

Source: gratisography.com

Great endings contain hope that change will lead to better outcomes for the readers. This is why shallow economic endings make crappy stories.

One of my favorite business stories comes from IBM when it sold off its hardware division because it realized the future was in software and services. IBM took a risk in doing this. The company went with the "Smarter Planet" initiative, which celebrated its role in making the future better by way of helping cities, government and businesses run "smarter" with software. The story resonated because it highlighted dramatic tension in the choice IBM faced. There were no margins in hardware, and IBM lost money rapidly. The company had no way to know if the "Smarter Planet" message would work. IBM was at a clear and very uncertain fork in the road: stay in a market that would not benefit the company or take a bold, uncertain risk and abandon hardware altogether. Both of these choices were uncertain and filled with risk. IBM chose the latter.

So while IBM projected optimism for a better future, the company was honest that that it could not do it alone. It needed to co-create the future together with partners. The company invited those partners to help write that future and story by being part of the initiative. The new story ended on an optimistic, though slightly uncertain note, and created a call to action: be part of a new story that we will build together. That's the power of optimism, co-creation, and a call to action in the face of uncertainty. It's also about the right balance of vulnerability in admitting and owning that uncertainty.

A Call to Action Needs an Appeal to Emotion

This story also highlights another key part to storytelling after conflict and change: a strong call to action. IBM invited partners to help shape the future of IBM and its story by helping to be part of the story. What do you want people to feel and do after your story? Think about that before you craft your story and think about what specific call to action you would like to make to your audience. Do you want them to share the story? Learn more by visiting your website? Advocate for a cause? Donate and share a video? Create content for your organization or share their story on your social media channels? Download a paper? Sign up for something? There are many options. It is important to decide that up front so you have a clear picture of what action you want them to take and what motivating feeling you want to leave them with.

Ending on an emotional note of personal change motivates more people to act on your story than a transactional message, as I mentioned in Chapter 4. People act when they are inspired to change, and they see a vision of how things could be different for them. Simply put, emotional story endings create motivational fuel that moves more people to act.

Conflict Can Come Earlier or Later, But it Must Come

Starting with "happy, healthy and well" as a story beginning is not a hard and fast rule. Once you understand the guidelines of storytelling and get good at them, you can play with and bend them a bit. Did you know Picasso painted like a Dutch Master before he experimented with cubism? He learned the best painting approaches that experts in his day studied then he experimented and flipped those models on their heads (which he probably drew with 10 eyes and 5 noses!)

You *can* jump right into the conflict or height of the action as a story beginning **as long as** we get to know the protagonist through the challenge he or she faces. The character must still be developed.

Conflict Takes Many Forms

All conflict can be powerful catalysts for change if it is specific enough for us to understand *why* it is a challenge and what is at stake for the protagonist if there is no resolution.

Conflict comes in many forms:

- External to the company (customers, partners, funding sources, competition, government regulations)
- Within the company (teams not getting along, personalities that don't see eye-to-eye, sexism or racism in the workplace)
- Within the protagonist (inner conflict – man vs. himself, or breaking through perceived limits put on one's self or by others)
- Personal issue / challenge (technology, health, spiritual, family, business need) that prompted protagonist to create a company in the first place or to make certain decisions and choices
- General economic / industrial challenge that affects all companies
- Institutionalized, larger social issues that affect business and people (racism, sexism, social injustices, the political landscape, economic forces, environmental issues such as clean water (and enough water), air pollution, etc.)

The source of the conflict does not matter as long as it's relevant to the business story, it's clear how it challenges the protagonist (personally and professionally), has emotional stakes, and creates change that allows audiences to walk away feeling optimistic.

Conflict works to help us identify with the story only when the character's wants are clear. Blocking a character from getting what he or she wants is a great and important source of tension. When characters are prevented from getting what they want, it raises the emotional stakes:

- What happens to the CEO who doesn't get funding?
- What happens to the Mompreneur who invests all of her money into bootstrapping her company if her product doesn't take off?
- What happens to the business owner who can't solve his or her IT challenges?
- What happens to the founder who has to lay people off?
- What happens to the CMO/CTO who can't scale customer service effectively?
- What happens to the small business that has a major client that doesn't pay and that's half of her revenue?

Creating Dramatic Tension: Provide Two Options

Source: gratisography.com

In addition to characters not getting what they want, another technique for creating dramatic tension is to highlight two choices a character faces. Tension happens when both choices are equally good, equally uncertain, or equally unappealing. When a character faces a choice between a good option and a not-so-good option, tension isn't heightened. It's clear which choice a rational character would make.

Yet, when the character faces two unknowns, two lousy choices, or two potentially great options, the choices become less clear. *That's* where dramatic tension can be heightened with great effect.

A great story doesn't need two options to create tension. However, if you want to build tension in your story, it's an effective way to do so.

Examples of Escalating Tensions

A CEO who has to lay off people or fold the company

An entrepreneur who has to sell the company to a majority investor with strings attached or take on a second, high-interest mortgage for funding

A company who has had a patent denied (or faces a patent lawsuit) and has lost its major customers must make the choice of carrying on alone with lots of liabilities or partner with a firm that wants a hostile takeover at a cheap price because of the assumed risk

A company or entrepreneur who is out of cash only to find out the product doesn't work the way it should. How will the company or person pivot?

"Today is the Day" Moments Raise Emotional Stakes

Choices create inflection points – where big decisions have to be faced, and thus, big changes are imminent.

If one choice is made, the scene goes one way; if another choice is made, the scene could go another way. There is no *right* choice, per se. While there are many possibilities in improvisation, inflection points are today-is-the-day moments where characters make big choices that can completely change the arc of the story. These are put-up or shut-up human moments that we all lean into while biting our nails because we've all faced these. And they raise the emotional stakes.

A few examples:

- Stay in a bad relationship or leave even though you care about the person;

- Take the job with an uncertain future or start your own company;
- Move to a new city and start something new not knowing anyone or stay in a dead-end job;
- Quit your crappy job and step out on your own even when you have a mortgage, spouse, two kids, and a pet (think: many startup stories!) or stay in your boring job with no prospects of a great future and get a regular paycheck

There are so many ways to go, and that's the beauty about inflection points. They are incredibly effective devices for adding tension and twists and turns that will make your stories so much better.

Tips Checklist

✓ What is the conflict in your story? Is it clear, specific, and real? Can your audience identify with it?
✓ Have you found a way to build tension in your story?
✓ Does your resolution demonstrate that peoples' lives have changed for the better? How? Remember hope and optimism! Change doesn't have to be big – even small change that is honest, relevant, and real makes a difference.

Conflict and change are two of the most important parts to a story. Too often, business storytelling eschews conflict because we're taught conflict is bad, vulnerable, and weak. Not so. Without a challenge to be overcome, we don't identify with the protagonist's plight. And challenge brings about that very important change we all want.

Next Up...

Coming up in chapter seven, we'll focus on a key tenet of improvisation: "Yes, and"-ing your partner and making them look good. That means making *them* the hero of the story on the business stage, too.

Source: Keepingithuman.com

7

HEY PARTNER, YOU'RE LOOKING GOOD

"The difference between a bad show and one that kills is that in the latter each improviser made someone else look good rather than being out for themselves. Focus on making sure your partner has a great show."
-Instructor at ComedySportz

Another key idea in improv is *make your partner look good.* Not that you need it. You already look amazing! Making your partner look good means supporting everything your scene partner says on stage. If she endows you as a mom for example, you "yes, and" that because everything your scene partner says is right.

In improv, your scene partner might say, "Mom, hand me the eggs."
You then say, "Ok, and drink your blood so you can be a strong vampire!"

So you "yes" the offer of being a mom *and* add on to it (the vampire choice in this case). Making your partner look good means "yes, and"-ing them and making sure whatever choice they make, you support as fact. (Side note: I did a great scene where I endowed myself as a werewolf and was then endowed by my partner as a mom. I was the best damn werewolf mom ever for the entire play).

In short, making your partner look good builds the 'we' and the 'us.' That's key because I mentioned earlier how important relationships are to remarkable scenes.

On stage, the only reality is what is created. There are no wrong choices; however, some choices are more ideal than others. You wouldn't stop your partner, break reality, and say, "Why did you say that?" That shuts your partner and scene down. Accepting everything your partner says as a gift to be added onto advances the story.

One of my favorite improvisation scenes I did (yes, I have a few) was when an improviser walked on stage and started shaking all around. I had no idea what he was doing, but one of the "rules" of improv is that you don't leave an improviser hanging out to dry in a scene. I walked on stage (because no dialogue can happen until there are two people out there) and did the exact same thing he was doing: shaking my legs, my arms, my torso, everything! The audience laughed. We looked at each other, nodded, and said nothing.

Pretty soon, another improviser joined us. We shook for what seemed to be 30-40 seconds without talking. We looked at each other, smiling and nodding, and shaking the entire time. The audience laughed, waiting patiently to see where we would go with the scene. Of course, so were those of us onstage. We laughed and continued shaking, not only to build tension, but also to figure out exactly who and what we were to each other because we didn't know right away.

Finally, the original improviser who had started the scene looked at both of us who had joined him onstage and exclaimed, "You know, being a Chihuahua sucks sometimes, right?" We responded with a resounding "Absolutely" and "God, yes." The audience went nuts. What a great choice! We found a way to create something from that tension and justified the scene. We simply supported each other with every comment and every action.

When you lend support to make another's big bold choice work, the output is far better than if each of us fought for attention for our individual ideas. That's the power of building something together.

Storytelling That Makes Others Look Good Builds Loyalty

In business storytelling, focusing on your partner means making someone else the hero while you become a key supporting character. This shift is significant because it means the best business storytelling is about *their* challenges and successes and how *they* become heroes to their organizations. Your company and products are not the focus. They are merely *enablers* to unleashing your customers' super-awesomeness! You are the Robin to *their* Batman.

Imagine the following stories:

- You are a bank. Instead of talking about your services, you talk about how your customer became a successful social entrepreneur. Of course, you provided funding.
- You are an enterprise software company, and you talk about how one of your customers (through the lens of a person – maybe a buyer or user) was able to use your software to grow leads 25%. Now she looks like a rock star to her CEO. Or, maybe one of your customers uses the technology to better match food banks with food supplies to reduce hunger in large urban communities.
- You are a nonprofit and your storytelling focuses on how you enabled one family to get back on their feet, financially, after the housing crisis. You profile a donor who used to be a client!
- Your healthcare products helped a customer manage diabetes better. As a result, he started a foundation to help other diabetics manage the disease and live productive lives.
- Your networking equipment allowed a fresh produce startup to successfully grow an ordering system. The business now serves more customers in low-income areas with fresh organic products.
- Your skincare products helped kids with eczema reduce flare-ups so they can feel normal again and not be teased.

Making your customer the hero means telling the story of your customers' successes, and by extension, how you helped in that process.

As you've read in other chapters, people buy results, optimism, and a better future. When you make your buyer the hero for their organization, your company / product / service becomes a powerful ally and supporting hero. And, you create a more loyal customer.

Focus your story lens on your partners and your employees, as well. They have great stories to share. Find the stories of ordinary people doing amazing things to help others, solve problems, and innovate for the right reasons.

Make Your Clients Look Good to Their Clients (Even Better: Make Your Clients' Clients Look Good!)

Years ago, I worked with a packaging company. Packaging is not a glamorous industry; yet, think about how vital it is to protecting items, to keeping them sanitary, and to keeping them from contamination. For certain goods, contamination renders those products unusable because they are unsafe. Sometimes when contamination happens, people don't realize it.

This packaging company had a few stories about themselves and very few stories told through the lens of its customers. So we did some digging. It turns out, packaging matters not just for items such as semiconductors. Packaging is critical for keeping items like catheters from contamination.

One of this company's clients was a catheter company. Catheters cause some of the highest infection rates in hospitals. Often, catheters become contaminated (unbeknownst to hospital staff) at the point of insertion. When a nurse, for example, inserts a catheter into a patient, he or she may be contaminating that product – and thus jeopardizing the safety of the patient – without even realizing it. This is a huge safety issue for hospitals. So anyone who could help catheter manufacturers reduce hospital infection rates would look like heroes to their clinic and hospital clients. And, in turn, this makes hospitals look good. If you can make your clients' clients look good, that's a tremendous testament to your value. We just got meta here.

Suddenly, that non-sexy packaging that helps your catheter clients makes their hospital clients look good by solving a real issue makes a wonderful story about making a real difference. This packaging company told the story of reducing infection rates through the lens of their client. Effective? Absolutely. And it shows that packaging isn't just protection for stuff we buy online but can be the difference between improved health or contracting an infection while your immune system is weakened. By focusing on making your partner look good (and their customers, too), your support story makes your product a vital part of that fight against illness and dangerous infections. Now, *that's* cool.

Tips Checklist

✓ Make your customer the focus of the challenge and success (with your help as an enabling tool).
✓ Focus on how your customer solves the challenge for *their* organization or was able to do something because of your service or achieve something elusive (even just feel normal) because of your products and services

✓ Focus on your sales partners (maybe you have partners in your business such as resellers, VARS, etc.)

✓ Focus on your employees being heroes of your organization: how they build products, communicate with others, share ideas to make customers' lives better. When employees are passionate brand advocates, your organization wins! And passionate employees are loyal and often are great storytellers with amazing tales to share. Involve them – they are more trusted as relatable, human faces of your company.

✓ Tell the best stories of your customers' customers through specific examples and people. That is a great testament to your company in terms of ability to add value.

Next Up…

Making others look good is a powerful way to build loyalty and trust with your employees, customers, and partners. And, yes, it is okay to be the hero of your own story – just not all the time. Coming up next, some final thoughts on humanizing storytelling by embracing the imperfect.

Source: Keepingithuman.com

8

EMBRACE IMPERFECTION

"Your goal is to be entertaining. To be in the audience and never see an improviser fail or make big bold choices is the most boring thing in the world. Screw up, be human, and react big. The same is true of characters you create for sketch comedy."
    -Instructor at Second City Sketch

People and Brands are Wonderfully Imperfect

Life is messy and imperfect. So are people. That's a beautiful thing because it is real. If you really want to connect with people, whether it's on a comedy or business stage, be a little vulnerable and embrace imperfection.

Source: gratisography.com

In improv, and, yes, even in business, some of the best moments are spontaneous, silly, unexpected "mistakes" that are gifts rather than failures. Improvisers sometimes break character and crack up. When we have fun on the stage, so does the audience. The best shows I have ever done—and I would suspect this is true for most performers—is when the players messed with each other, cracked each other up, made mistakes, and then tried to work through them to create a cogent story. The audience loves seeing the humanity in imperfection. And vulnerable characters make people say, "That is me!"

Imperfect is funny. Years ago, one of my improv friends, Chris, had to be "Hannah Montana" in a scene. (For those not in the know – this was the breakout Disney Channel role that made Miley Cyrus a household name in her early teens). He was endowed with that character at the suggestion of the audience. At that time, Chris was a 40-year-old single guy who had no idea who Hannah Montana or Miley Cyrus was. He was an improv player at a birthday party for a 13-year-old girl and about 30 of her friends and family members who filled the theater on this particular evening. They paid to see a show, and what they wanted was to see a big, hairy grown man play Hannah Montana.

My friend Chris is a talented improviser who says, "yes" to everything. He said to the audience laughingly and honestly, "I am a 40-year-old single guy who doesn't know the suggestion." The girls laughed hysterically and starting chanting "Hannah, Hannah, Hannah!" Was it going to be perfect? Hell no. But it was going to be brilliantly funny because with that contrast, how could it not be? I slapped a blonde wig on him and gave him a few pointers about the alter-ego singer. He knew little more than that he had to keep taking off the wig to be Miley Cyrus. Wig on and, voilà: instant Hannah Montana! And you have to do lots of singing. That's all he knew as he was pushed to the stage.

With those two pieces of information, this slightly heavy, 40-year-old, hairy guy with a blonde wig sang nonsense lyrics and took his wig off. A lot. To say it was hilarious is an understatement. The contrast had the audience in stitches. Had he known who the character was and played it really close to her to be more accurate, the performance would not have been as funny. Watching this big guy who clearly didn't know the character try to be the character was brilliant beyond measure. He *fully committed* to the role. He got everything wrong, but the audience clapped and shouted gleefully from their seats. Being bold, brave and completely imperfect was what made this scene work. I remember it all these years later and I still tease Chris about it.

Brand Storytelling is Better When it's a Little Imperfect

Businesses don't have to go all out like Chris did. However, brands are imperfect and are often unwilling to show their imperfections in the stories they tell. Businesses are so afraid of appearing imperfect that their stories become unemotional and boring. Perfection is like a platinum shade of blonde— it doesn't exist in nature. For a lot of companies and brands it's scary because it means being a little vulnerable. No one expects you to be perfect and news flash: none of your customers think you are! That's the good news.

Source: gratisography.com

Embrace imperfection in your business storytelling and make it work for you so your audience connects with you emotionally. Here are a few key ideas to focus on:

- **Your characters and mistakes**. Show your mistakes and foibles in your stories and on social media. Talk about the failures as key turning points for your business. The point isn't to focus on the failure; rather, it is to show what you learned and how you grew from it. Most "overnight" successes, for example, weren't. It may be a 10-years-in-the-making story. Just as you anchor other stories through a human lens (which we talked about already), your mistakes and failure stories should also be anchored through a human lens. A failure story of 'the company did this and that' doesn't pass the vulnerability and human tests. If you go there, and it can be really powerful, a mistake or failure story should be told through the founders' lenses or the head of product or the CEO. Or it could be through a product developer or any employee. The point is to make it real. That's where the credibility boost happens.

- **Tell us about the highs and lows in the journey and how it grew you and your business**. I made many mistakes in my business journey. When I first started, I knew marketing, and I knew comedy. I didn't know how to run a business. I first went after small businesses because I had affection for them because I was a small business, and they needed my services, right? They did, but they didn't want to pay for sales and marketing. Many small businesses, therefore, fail from a lack of sales and marketing. And if I didn't change my ideal audience for my services, I, too, was going to be a nonprofit. I learned so much from this stage of my business that it made my business – and me – better. I tell this story because it taught me so much. I pass those lessons on. Failures are amazing learning experiences, so focus on what they taught you and how you used those lessons to make positive changes.

- **Who hasn't failed?** I live in Silicon Valley, the epicenter of technology. I can say this having come from high-tech marketing: if you have lived and worked in technology and you don't have a failed startup in your resume somewhere, many people will wonder whether you took any career risks. It's not a human failure when it made you better. Share those stories to inspire and remind your audience they are not alone. Failure is part of the human journey.

- **Your choices**. Life often has imperfect choices. The best we can do is make choices from the hand we're dealt. In an earlier chapter, I mentioned that tension is heightened when the choices in front of us are uncertain. Share the uncertainty you felt and how those stories played out. What did you learn, and how did they shape the path you are now on? If you do the digging and analysis, you will find that most experiences, no matter how painful or uncertain, helped shape you in some positive way. Sharing your choices and what you learned helps others.

- **Your story endings**. Business stories that go for perfect endings often backfire. It's not the way things work in most peoples' lives. It is far better to tell a simple story with an honest, imperfect ending than try to tie everything up with an exaggerated bow. *Hopeful* doesn't need to be perfect. An honest, optimistic ending in your stories still provides hope that your audience can see better futures for themselves. If you are in the process of reinventing yourself, share that story with your audience. Let them know that your ending is still being written. Most audiences will relate to that. We're all works in progress, as people and as businesses.

Co-Create with Others Who Carry the Story Flame for You

You are not expected to have all the answers in your business stories. One really great way to embrace imperfection and create better narratives is to invite your audience to co-create with you. Let them help shape your narrative in a way that is even better. Look at brands like Tough Mudder, GoPro, IBM, Salesforce, and Intel, among others. They tell much of their story through the lens of customers and partners. Much of their content is co-created or created outside company walls. And even inside company walls. IBM, for example, has thousands of employee bloggers who share their employee stories.

When improvisers co-create on a stage, the results are far better than if one improviser drove every scene and choice. The same thing can be true of co-created narratives where you invite your audiences to share their stories, build onto yours, or shape your endings. Here are a few ways to invite participation in your business storytelling and scale your efforts in a powerful way beyond what you can achieve alone:

- **Write a better (more real) ending by inviting others to help.** When companies rebrand or reinvent themselves, there is uncertainty, fear, and doubt about how that will play out. Being open with your audience is powerful. Strategy is often made on imperfect information. That means there is always some risk. Invite your audience to help you create new ideas, new products, and new stories for your business. As mentioned in the last chapter, IBM did this when it sold off its hardware business because there were no margins anymore. It shifted gears, doubled-down on this new story, and told the market exactly why it believed this was the best route for IBM's future. And it invited partners to help tell their stories, shape the larger smarter planet narrative and be part of something bigger than IBM. It was a joint story and an open invitation to collaborate. As partners told stories about their role in IBM's new business, IBM grew. They focused on making their partners look good! More recently, as of this writing, IBM is experiencing more changes. Things change frequently. For all of us.

- **Let your best employee storytellers loose.** With the right training and some guidance, your best storytellers will tell a more human version of the company narrative through their experiences. Passionate employees are credible, compelling, and convincing. Usually, the best storytellers are not in the C-Suite. Often times, they are not in the marketing department; rather, they are the people closest to the customers—those employees on the front lines of service and customer experiences. One of my favorite examples is about Cisco's rapping intern. He was a Stanford University intern who would rap about working for Cisco and invite other interns to rap about their corporate internship experiences. His videos got lots of engagement and were big with Gen Y audiences Cisco wanted to reach. Cisco went with it because even then-CEO John Chambers recognized that corporate marketing could never have produced that same authentic connection.

- **Let your customers and partners tell their stories their way**. Invite your customers to tell their stories in their way without your marketing filter. Customer-created stories and content are more credible and usually far more creative (not drowning in corp-speak!), and, thus, more widely shared. Think: Tough Mudder, GoPro, and even SAP where community and customer content make up a large percent of the content the companies use in their marketing.

Whew! You made it through the first part of this book. Go buy yourself something nice. You earned it.

Source: gratisography.com

Before you do take that well-deserved break, however, let's review everything you've done. The first part of this book was about how to take concepts from the improvisation stage and use them on the business storytelling page (and stage)! Techniques such as narrative arcs, conflict, tension, change, focusing on your partner and making them the hero, embracing imperfection, and highlighting every character's needs and wants increase the emotional cohesiveness of your business story. The human quotient will always be the spark of your business storytelling, and it will help you banish boring.

You are amazing, and your stories should be amazing, too!

Next Up...

In the second part of the book, we'll focus on using improv-based exercises (adapted from games we play onstage) to generate content marketing ideas. These activities can also be used to generate new business models, sales processes, product and service ideas, and concepts for your branding team. That's the power of improv-infused marketing: it can be applied to many things!

On the next page is a worksheet with improv tips we've covered for humanizing your business stories and kicking boring in the pants!

Go take that break and get ready to have some fun generating ideas (I call them idea orgasms!) in part II.

SUMMARY 'HUMAN-STORY' WORKSHEET

Here is a summary checklist for humanizing your business storytelling (and banishing boring!) whatever purpose you are creating stories for. We covered all these things in the first half of this book. If you follow many of these tips, you'll see improvements immediately.

Clear Objectives

• What do you want people to feel and do (what action do you want them to take) after hearing the story?

Start with that end in mind first. Get beyond the transaction.

Defined Characters

• Who is the protagonist? (A person, not a company)
• What does he/she want? What is the human need?
• What unique point of view does this character have?
• What unique mannerisms or traits add to the story?
• How does he or she feel about things as the story moves on?
• Is the character imperfect or does the character exhibit empathy if demonstrating that is part of the objective of the story? Show us. Make us feel it.

Be sure to add color (depth) where appropriate so we identify with the character. Give specific details about the character, his or her world, point of view, and how emotions change.

Setting Specifics

• What is the environment?
• What does it smell like? Sound like? Look like?
• How does it add to the situation and to what the character is feeling?

Relevant details can add to the emotions your readers experience.

The Human Challenge

- What is the challenge / inciting incident?
- How does that challenge appear in a human way so that your audience can relate to it (that means the human want should be clear!)?
- How is the character blocked from getting a need met?
- How does this challenge affect the character?
- Why does it matter?

What is at stake if the need is not met?

Rising Tension and Climax

- What adds to the tension in the story?
- Are there uncertain or hard choices the character must make (inflection points)?
- How does tension build to a head? Are there equally bad or uncertain choices?
- Can you add more commentary/action to the plot?
- For comic effect (optional and it works in certain contexts): heighten the conflict by showing the character getting blocked in a benign way and still not giving up.

Resolution

- How is the tension resolved?
- What happens?
- What's the new "status quo" after the resolution?

Change

- How does the resolution change the character?
- How does the character feel by the end?
- How does the resolution change the character's world?
- Where is the hope and optimism beyond the transaction?

Source: Keepingithuman.com

PART II:

Idea Orgasms! Improv Exercises to Innovate 'Boring-Busting' Marketing Ideas

Source: gratisography.com

9

IDEA ORGASMS! IMPROV EXERCISES TO UNLEASH YOUR CREATIVE AWESOME

This chapter is going to rock your socks off. Or your superhero footsie pajamas! I say that for a "friend." This section will give you some easy, fun, doable ways to get unstuck, generate super-creative new ideas, and change the way you approach content and story idea generation. *Side note:* I'd say "ideation" but then I'd break my own rule against "jargon-monoxide" (you know, ridiculous business jargon as I call it!), and have to kick my own butt. "Idea orgasms" sounds way better.

These exercises will help you get unstuck. What I absolutely love about these activities is that they can be used for more than content and story idea generation. I have used most to also generate product and service ideas, customer service improvements, branding ideas, business model and sales process innovations, and more. I even used them recently to help a tech company generate new ways to reach out to and recruit more Millennials. How cool is that? Improv-based techniques work, and they strengthen your creative core!

Tips for Taking it All In

As you read this chapter, pick at least two exercises that resonate most with you and do them right away. Adapt for your needs. Experiment soon after you read this, while your curiosity and willingness to experiment are raring to go.

As explained, improv centers around a "yes, and" mentality because "Yes, but" shuts people down. And, as I have often said, *"A 'yes, but' is really a 'no' parading in cheap perfume and costume jewelry."*

"Yes, and" embraces playfulness and possibility. There is a place for narrowing ideas and whittling the remainder down into actionable steps based on viability. That is the **probability** spectrum of the funnel, and that comes at a later stage. The beginning of the idea process is about possibility, and it is the widest part of your funnel. So allow "yes, and" to fill the top of your funnel with great ideas.

Possibility--Probability
(You are here!)   **IDEA   FUNNEL**   **(You'll get here soon!)**

Top 10: How You Know Your Brainstorming Meeting Sucks

According to researchers[ix], there are over 11 million business meetings that happen in America every day. It feels like I have been in every single one of them because most meetings, especially brainstorming ones, aren't very good. And I know you probably feel the same way! Here are 10 ways you know your brainstorming is a bust:

10. People are texting each other during the meeting.
9. There is an agenda no one read that was put together by the one person who loves meetings. Note: never give this person power!
8. HR uses "mandatory" and "FUN" together, putting the "FU" in Fun.
7. One person makes up an excuse to leave then pops up at the end of the meeting and has done nothing. Who the hell is this person?
6. People call your brainstorming session, "Ideation." Jargon-monoxide poisoning attack! Run!
5. Your facilitator, who might actually be a robot, breaks every rule about good facilitation. Now you feel that's unfair...to robots!
4. Every idea you try to give results in a "yes, but..."
3. You want to hurt your team members, and you are not violent.
2. You have someone who judges every idea because she thinks that's her self-appointed job and doesn't contribute any herself.
1. People stop trying because a few jerks say, "That will never work!"

A Few Ground Rules

(These are important, and you don't want to skip. Skipping for fun is good, though. You should totally do that.)

- No judging yourself or others' ideas.

"Never, ever judge your own journey. That's what family is for."

-Kathy Klotz-Guest

Source: Kathy Klotz-Guest

- Keep going until you can't go anymore
- Go beyond the obvious. That may mean warming up for a few minutes and feeling like you aren't getting there *before* the good stuff happens (after a few minutes, the spigot will run!)
- Yes, and: add onto what's been said. Don't question it or comment on its viability. Viability doesn't matter at the early stages.
- Like any methodology you use, not all ideas will be viable. If you

go past the obvious stuff, you will unearth new ideas.

- Have fun! Be playful. Unleash your inner kid. It knows best. Except when it comes to eating too much candy. Hide the candy first.

Now your team is ready to trust each other, laugh, and enjoy the process! You can do these, solo, too, and still get great results.

Improv Activities You Can Use Anytime, Anywhere

Below is a list of exercises I'll explain individually and you can see my YouTube channel[x] (https://www.youtube.com/c/KathyKlotzGuest) for more videos I will be adding over time.

Life is like the hokey-pokey.
Don't half-ass it.
Put your whole ass in.
And shake it all about.

That's what it's all about.

-Kathy Klotz-Guest

Source: Keepingithuman.com

There are many more exercises beyond what I have listed below (21 in total). All but two (that came from my improv group) exist as public domain games designed for the improv stage and they come from

119

different places in the community. These are some of my favorites. I have adapted them from their raw stage form to work for my needs in business. *What I have in this book are my specific modifications (made and tested over years), and directions on how I apply them to business (vs. their raw, pure game form which is what you will typically find online).* I also note the two below that came from my improv team as new games for our shows. I now use them in my work, and you can, too.

- *Fortunately, Unfortunately*
- *Yes, and!*
- *Combining Passions*
- *Finding Similarities Between Dissimilar Objects*
- *Object Reinvention*
- *Caption That! (Note: This is an activity my improv group created)*
- *Forward/Reverse (Note: My adaptation is Think Backwards)*
- *Replay*
- *If That is True, What Else is True?*
- *I Like That and…*
- *Role Reversals*
- *Status Shifts*
- *Day in the Life (of Your Brand!)*
- *What Happens Next?*
- *Clash of Contexts/Fish Out of Water*
- *50 Titles in 5 Minutes (or less)*
- *I Kissed a…*
- *Stream of Consciousness (really good for getting unstuck)*
- *What are You Doing? (Really good for getting unstuck)*
- *Motivational Poster (my improv group created it as a game)*
- *Motivational Poster with Irony*

Exercise 1: Fortunately, Unfortunately

Great uses: getting unstuck, warming up, seeing the possibility in any situation, idea generation for products, content, events, and more. Using this activity, I helped a credit union come up with new marketing events and promotions. I also used this exercise with a few improve friends to help a company with a tea product uncover funny ways to market its product. Humor works! This exercise is best in a group situation, although you can do it solo.

This exercise is designed to help you get past the obvious stuff that happens when we sit down to brainstorm. The first few minutes feel like all our ideas are pretty basic. They can be. With all of these approaches, keep going until you find your creative groove. As Dory in *Finding Nemo* optimistically says, "Keep swimming, swimming, swimming!"

Channeling that same optimism here, this exercise forces your brain to reframe things that might be thought of as a negative or obvious into a positive. This changes the wiring in your brain so that when you are handed what looks like a tough card, you can choose to reframe that set of circumstances or marketing mishap into something positive with opportunity.

How it Works: The first person starts out with "Fortunately." Then, it alternates: the next person does "Unfortunately." And you alternate (one person does fortunately, the next person unfortunately, the next does fortunately (you get the point) until you are done. Go past the first three minutes. At first, it may feel a little new, weird, and different. It doesn't mean you are doing it wrong. In fact it *should* feel a little foreign at first.

Start with a pain point for your customer or perhaps a new campaign suggestion. Or start with a premise about your customer and what they want. The important thing is to start with a specific statement or specific idea of what you want to improve. You are looking for new ways to think about your service, your campaign, new content ideas, or new product ideas. Record the session so you get all the really good ideas down. Some of these will be viable and some won't. Don't worry about deciding which category suggestions fall into now.

Example

Fortunately, we have a new service that allows Millennials to save money with our bank and get free gifts for every $200 saved.

Unfortunately, our competition is thinking of something similar. And we need to differentiate.

FFoorrttuunnaatteellyy, we have tied this to specific causes that allow Millennials to donate to organizations they choose if they don't want to keep the money. Also, we have a savings plan that lets them save based on frequent purchases they make. We think this will differentiate us.

Unfortunately, we don't have enough participation in those causes yet.

Fortunately, we can enlist our ideal clients who are active to help us market with social media and we can learn from them.

Unfortunately, we don't know what causes they want most.

Fortunately, we do know that a large percent of our Millennial customers love music and pets, and we could have a pet and music fair for them to get them to learn how to save and donate more. It could be part education, part networking, and a lot of fun. We just have to create compelling content around it and get Millennials to help spread the word! And we can use this event to get more educated about their specific needs.

Unfortunately, we don't have the space to hold these events.

Fortunately, we could have it at a public park nearby and encourage customers to bring their pets. That would make it more "friendly" and less formal "business event" driven — and we do know that demographic prefers more fun and casual events.

And you could keep going on for a while. If you do, you should continue until you get to some really amazing ideas. And you will. The point is to extend the comment that came before. Address the negatives and turn them into opportunities.

By doing this exercise (abbreviated here for space), we uncovered a few things:

1) That Millennials want to donate, want to be educated on financial matters, and that they love pets, networking and music. So we could

create **campaigns and content** around pets, music and donations if we were a bank or credit union. You could even create a new service or product at the bank that allows Millennials to save money when they buy things or donate to animal causes or music foundations.

2) In addition to using ideas for campaigns, products, and content, you could have **in-person events** to bring people together around those topics in order to learn more and create value for your customers. One avenue we uncovered includes networking events with pets to bring Millennials together to meet each other, educate each other (and be educated) on areas of saving, on entrepreneurship and on social entrepreneurship subjects including animal causes. Most importantly, these events should be casual, informal and fun!

As you get going, lots of new ideas will emerge! Some of them will be fresh, bold, and very doable.

Your Turn: Go for 5-6 Minutes. You got this.

Exercise 2: Yes, and!

Great uses: getting unstuck, warming up, idea generation for new products, content, events, branding, and customer experience design. With this activity, I helped employees at a large network equipment company design new product ideas, recruiting tactics, and blog content. I also helped to create content for a coaching services company. This is ideal in a group of two or more. While you can do it solo, it can be challenging alone. Part of the beauty of a group is that others will see things you don't. That's the power of collaboration.

In this exercise, you will add onto what has come before you. That means, your partner (or you) will make a statement and you will accept that statement and then *add* onto it.

Source: visualpun.ch by CC 2.0[xi]

How it Works: You will say, "Yes, and (add on something new)" after each statement. It's really important to take that idea further rather than just say "yes" or take the idea in a different direction. You are building onto each other's ideas. Each person does this by adding on. Try to go for at least 5 minutes.

Example

Let's suppose you are a small business that helps other small businesses stay motivated (maybe you are a business coach, for the sake of being specific). Perhaps you feel like you don't have time to create new content (or maybe you are out of ideas) and you barely have enough time to get exercise. You are overloaded and looking for ways to create content in your busy life that is fresh and different for your users. And you would also like to spend more time on self-care, but self-care keeps you from spending time on content. You are struggling to do it all. Your goal (always be specific) is to create fresh content to motivate people with new ideas and inspiration; and, if possible, find ways to take care of yourself, too.

Let's jump in (have someone else "yes, and" you...or, if alone, "yes, and" yourself):

Start with a specific statement: I need more content, and I can create more content by repurposing what I have.

Yes, and we could add videos because videos are in demand and entertaining.

Yes, and videos don't take a lot of time to make, especially if we just talk conversationally to the camera.

Yes, and we could make videos of things we are already doing and maybe we could also get video outside because nature inspires. And that wouldn't require lots of resources and editing time if we don't get too fancy and just concentrate on great content.

Yes, and we could get more exercise as we video our walks; and as we walk, we could talk to our audience to inspire them to also go walking and get in touch with their thoughts that way.

Yes, and we could pick different topics every few days just for a few minutes to motivate people to get out there and take breaks and get into nature.

Yes, and we could invite interesting people on our walks and video our chats so we can have different guests inspire others. These can be walking interviews.

Yes, and we could challenge our viewers to develop walking and talking brain trust groups, too. This way, they can support each other, get exercise together at the same time, and generate content ideas for their own businesses. They can also video their walking talks!

Yes, and as we walk, we could talk about ways to stay motivated then share all this great content with our audience. Our audiences can also share their videos with others. We could ask them to share their creations with us and form a community of support.

Yes, and it takes little additional work to create spontaneous videos of our conversations that we will do anyway. And with little editing work, we have content that humanizes the entrepreneur journey, inspires people to think differently by getting outside, and reminds people to get out, talk to others, share, commune in nature and get exercise.

If you look at what happened above, by accepting (saying "YES") to every idea *and* adding onto it (our "and") we unleashed a creative flow of ideas. We got into an upwardly positive idea spiral. Idea orgasm! How many of these ideas are doable? Lots of them, I think. Many of these are low-cost or free because they require very little in the way of resources to execute.

And the best part is that we found ways for this coach to motivate, create new content, build community by walking with others, and deepen relationships at the same time. What's even better is that everyone gets outside into nature and gets exercising, enabling the further flow of creative ideas. Now that is inspiring, motivating, and viable!

It's a virtuous creative cycle—the creative gift that keeps on giving. And that is how and why "yes, and" can be so powerful.

Your Turn: *"Yes and"* **in teams or try this exercise for 5 minutes** or until you run out of ideas! Pick a specific issue to "yes and" first. The more specific you are, the better the results will be.

Exercise 3: Combine Passions or Ideas (Mash-Ups!)

Great uses: warming up, idea generation for new products, content, events, branding, and customer experience design. I used this activity at a number of tech, consumer, and financial companies to create new service ideas with product teams and uncover new content ideas (blog posts, downloads, and videos) for marketing teams. While it is ideal for groups, you can do it alone by combining your own interests or products to make something new. I use it all the time! At a conference I spoke at near the time this book was being finished, attendees created ideas including fish monocles, nudist singing tacos (burrito bowls are really just naked burritos or tacos!), running sprint/shopping races, and a French motorcycle cooking club. The last one the group was going to turn into video content for their cooking site! So this stuff does yield fun, great ideas.

Source: gratisography.com

This exercise is one of my favorites. Ok, it's true - I love all these exercises (mostly) equally as if they were my kids! This exercise can help you see new ideas by combining things in new ways. Your brain loves mash-ups, and we all take things and find new ways to put them together, consciously or unconsciously, every day. It's another way to flex and develop those creative muscles. Think how great mash-up songs are. Especially when you take two or more awesome things and combine them! So many innovations and ideas today involve things that are not completely new to the world – they are combinations and adaptations of things that already exist and the a-ha is in the way they are combined to form something new and interesting.

How it Works: In this exercise, start by picking a passion or interest of your organization (you can also take an idea or a prior content piece or product and combine it with others). So if you are a ride-sharing service, as an example, one of your passions might be reducing the environmental footprint of a community.

Next, find a key passion of your users. What do they care about? So, based on your research online, from a survey or on comments shared in your community and on social media, you should have a sense of your users' priorities—the environment, social entrepreneurship, travel, animals, technology, whatever it is.

Example

Suppose that one large interest for your users is animals. You discover a large percent of your user base has pets. That is specific. **Big note: in this example, I am only using two passions. You can do this exercise combining three or more passions into a new service or campaign idea. I have done it, and it's a blast. Start with two mash-ups, then add three, and then see if you can add more and integrate them all into something new.**

You can approach this exercise several ways:

1. **To develop new content ideas**. Start with your company's passion around reducing the environmental footprint in the community and combine it with a passion your users share (in this case we are using pets/animals) to see how many content ideas you generate combining these passions. Jumping in, some of those mash-ups might involve the following opportunities:

   ✓ Humorous video about ride-sharing for pets
   ✓ Campaign around community enrichment with public pet birthday parties

✓ Company "pets day." Allow people to bring their pet to work and make employee vids for a marketing campaign
✓ Ride-sharing employees and drivers dress as their favorite animals with contests for passengers. Ask your users to record and share their content from this day

2. **Another great way to use this exercise is to come up with new services** for your company by combining those passions

✓ Ride-sharing for pets
✓ Let users bring their pets in the cars with them (maybe for a day or for a special fee)
✓ Pet birthday parties shuttle services
✓ Networking events for ride-sharing customers at SPCA locations or pet stores (could be a campaign, too)
✓ Community events and free rides on those days (could be a campaign, too)

Your Turn: Take 5 minutes! Take one passion of your company and one passion you know a high percent of your users share. Combine the two in new ways. Write ideas on a whiteboard. Or, speak a 5-minute stream of consciousness into a recording device or smartphone. See what ideas surface. Rinse and repeat. Take it back to work with you and use this method with your teams later. Tell me what results you get. I am excited for what you will uncover.

Exercise 4: Find Similarities Between Dissimilar Objects

Great uses: getting unstuck, idea generation for new products, content, branding, customer experience design, and marketing and sales processes. I used this with sales teams to come up with storytelling ideas, and I used it with a branding team that wanted to streamline its brand to appeal to a new audience. From there, we created content ideas. I also used it with a bank that wanted to improve its customer service processes. It works for those things, too.

This is another version of a Mash-Up where our brains love putting things together that, on the surface, appear to be very dissimilar. Yet, the more we find similarities between objects or ideas that appear to be different, the more similarities we see (our brains like to assimilate things) and we actually create new neural pathways. The more you do it, the better you get at it. How cool is that? Creative weight training for your brain without the silly headbands and spandex!

This is also a great exercise to do when you are looking for inspiration on almost anything.

How it Works: You take two objects or ideas that seem from different worlds and you try to see the similarities by relating them.

Big Tips for making this easier: You can take two objects and relate them, or an abstract thing and one object. I have learned doing this that **you will want to use at least ONE object in the exercise**. Physical objects have tangible attributes that you can relate to other ideas and objects. Using two abstract ideas can be challenging. Also, it does not matter what object you choose. Part of the exercise is to see similarities, and you will be able to do that with almost any object. A *glass Coke bottle*, for example in this exercise, has the following attributes that we can list:

- ✓ Is transparent, clear
- ✓ It has a shape that narrows at the middle
- ✓ It has a narrow opening and a wide bottom
- ✓ It has a weight to it because of the glass
- ✓ It has a cap that has to be taken off
- ✓ Its contents have a distinct smell
- ✓ It has a trademark shape and logo recognizable anywhere

Example

For this example, we ask a question (and be specific about the challenge – that's key here): *How can we make our content marketing more like this classic hour-glass shaped Coke bottle?* Here, you are trying to relate your marketing to a random object in order to generate ideas on how you could improve your content marketing process:

- ✓ It's narrow at the top and wide in the middle. We need to make our marketing wider at the top of the funnel if we want to move more people to the middle part. We will need more targeted content and campaigns focused on the right segments and we must reduce the percent of prospects lost between the top and wider middle part of the funnel.
- ✓ It's transparent, as we'd like our marketing process to be more transparent with customers. Let's ask them for ideas and improve communication with them.
- ✓ It's a bit heavy and we'd like to reduce our overhead in the outbound and inbound approaches. So let's identify ways to do this.
- ✓ It has a recognizable shape, and we'd like our content to be more recognizable with our distinct voice. Therefore, we need to sharpen our marketing so it could be picked out of a content line-up among the competition.

Example Two

Let's take a ball-point pen and relate it to how we can make our storytelling better. First, list the physical attributes of a pen. It has:

- ✓ Ink
- ✓ A point
- ✓ Color
- ✓ Cap
- ✓ Slender
- ✓ Has a clip for pockets
- ✓ Clickable
- ✓ Fancy writing / logo
- ✓ Sits in a gold holder

Now, let's list all the ways these can inspire better storytelling and different ways to tell stories:

- ✓ Our storytelling needs to make really clear points and have calls to action. So will add stronger calls to action on all our written and video stories.
- ✓ Like the pen, we could have stories be clickable or interactive, where users could share their own stories.
- ✓ We could cap the number of stories we generate every month and instead feature campaigns designed by users, or let users "cap" the stories we tell by creating their own endings. This way, we engage the users and invite them to participate.
- ✓ We could make our stories shorter – more slender like a pen, and make more serial episodes of them.
- ✓ We could create pocket-sized books of our brand stories that inspire people to create their own brand stories.

Your Turn: Try to Go for 5 Minutes. Try to relate specific attributes to your campaign, product, process, whatever so that you can ask yourself, *"How can these identifiable object attributes improve our process, campaign, content, business model, or product?"* That's why **specific attributes** help.

Be sure to frame the challenge specifically up front, so you know what specific elements relate to those physical attributes.

Source: gratisography.com

132

Exercise 5: Object Reinvention

Great uses: getting unstuck, warming up, idea generation for new products, content, events, branding, customer experience design, and improved customer service. I use this one with many clients to start the idea process and then we do a round of "Yes, and" on top of some of the results they get from this exercise. For a healthcare company and a packaging company, I used this method with teams. We generated lots of new video, blog, and story ideas. We also came up with new customer service ideas. The teams had a great time. This activity works well in teams, but it is also an exercise you can do alone first and then combine with someone else.

This is a super fun game I use all the time with clients, in my own work, and with my 7-year-old. I know from experience it brings out the inner kid in any adult. I typically use this game with client teams to *start* the creative flow of ideas, just to get the spigot going.

Source: gratisography.com

How it works: Take any object. I like to start by using my client company's product as a starting point, but it does not have to be. So if I work with an app company, for instance, we start with an app. If they make hardware, start with that. If you don't produce a tangible product, that's okay. Take your service. It's a bit easier thinking of your product in tangible terms; yet, it's not a deal breaker by any means, to start with an intangible. It just means you have to work a little differently and spend a bit more time to get past the obvious things. And physical products tend to be slightly easier.

Remember Avon's *Skin So Soft* product? Well, that bath liquid designed to soften the skin (and it did work) also made a fabulous insect repellant! As another example, baking soda doubles as a teeth-whitening agent. One never knows what innovations might happen as a collision of ideas when we realize that products and services can often be used for things other than what they were originally designed for.

Example

If your company makes shoes, start by generating as many ideas for ways you could use shoes other than on your feet. **Remember, you are looking for something** *other* **than what your product or service was specifically designed for**. Instead of shoes, this "object" is turned into:

- ✓ Slobber catcher
- ✓ Instant Faux Hawk
- ✓ Hand warmers
- ✓ Spider catchers
- ✓ Bath toys
- ✓ Sleds for mice
- ✓ Beds for mice
- ✓ Planters
- ✓ Key holders
- ✓ Pen holders
- ✓ Makeup receptacles
- ✓ Pin cushions
- ✓ Chia Pet holders
- ✓ Painted art installation
- ✓ Rubber band holder
- ✓ Mobile spice racks
- ✓ Paper weight
- ✓ Jewelry container
- ✓ Cat or dog chew toy (which I guess it is, anyway!)

Keep going. You will find yourself on a roll.

Do the same if you have a service. Maybe you offer a ride-sharing service. Ask yourself, *"what other things could we offer / do with our drivers (your product) besides ride-sharing (which is already our primary business)?"* Some ideas might include:

- ✓ Food pick-up and delivery
- ✓ Mobile network access (people get inside for great Wi-Fi)
- ✓ Mobile dating (people meet and converse in the car on a date while driver drives around the city)
- ✓ Mobile speed-dating (even better – you get 10 minutes and then time's up. Out of the car, bucko!)
- ✓ Mobile poetry slams
- ✓ Mobile food tasting services
- ✓ Mobile chefs: Have local chefs give free samples on location
- ✓ Mobile library where you sit in the car and check out books
- ✓ Mobile coffee house (sit in and drink) and/or coffee delivery
- ✓ Mobile air-conditioning for hot summer months

Part II: Some of these ideas might make great marketing videos and / or be the germ of a new product idea, a fun post or a marketing promotion.

When you are looking for content ideas, look at your list and see what sticks out as something that would provide value to your audience.

If you are shoemaker or seller (or sustainability company, environmental services organization, or even a municipal recycling service) and looking for great new content ideas, consider a post on how to reuse old shoes rather than throw them away (a great way to cut down on shoes in a landfill, assuming they are not in shape to be donated). That's high value, fresh, and different. Think of five easy ways to recycle and re-use your old worn-out shoes and create content around that. Or, perhaps a post on what your customers have done with their old shoes could help create great user-generated content and community engagement around a shared passion for repurposing and caring for the environment. Even better!

If you're a ride-sharing service, what topics could be interesting as content to your audience? Going back to the list we generated above as a starting point, you identify that you could create an article on the best places to eat in every neighborhood you service (again, in this example you are a ride-sharing service) with reviews by ride-sharing drivers or customers who live there. Go beyond just ride-sharing. *Now you are in the idea-sharing business, and that expands possibilities.*

There's no end to what you can do. Allow yourself to go to as many places as possible until you run out of steam. When you start to slow down and repeat ideas, you most likely have a great starting list. As a further step, you can identify individual items or combine items from your generated list (like we did before) to create even more new marketing ideas.

Boom! There you go! You are cooking now. Let's keep going.

Your Turn. Go for 10 minutes as you and your team generate new ideas for alternate ways your product or service could be used.

Exercise 6: Caption That! (My improv team came up with this one and it cracks up audiences)

Great uses: getting unstuck, idea generation for content headlines, big story ideas, and product ideas. I use this one a lot for my own business and for clients that are testing big ideas to see how they sound in a tight headline. I do this activity solo when I am brainstorming by myself; however, I find it ideal in small teams.

I adapted this game to help teams come up with great headlines and ideas for posts. In a brainstorm session by yourself or with your team, as you discuss content, it's important to think of the big headline (the big a-ha!) you want your customer to walk away with. So, if you create content around helping customers reduce their carbon footprint, you should be able to create one big headline for your article, your infographic, other image, eBook, or whatever you are producing, around that single big idea. That headline needs to be bold. Example: *10 Big, Stress-Free Ways You Can Save the Environment Today!*

Come up with the big headline first and create content around that.

How it Works: As people pitch ideas, I stop them and say 'caption that,' so as to leave a big, bold visual image in the customer's mind. It forces your team members to distill that idea into the one big, bold, attention-grabbing takeaway. Want some inspiration? Look at BuzzFeed headlines, or titles from Upworthy! After someone says, "Caption That!" to an idea, the person who has the idea steps forward and has to give the big, newsworthy headline. If they cannot articulate a big, bold headline, the idea likely needs more work. It also helps you frame and focus your content through a lens you know will grab your customer.

If you can't quite get the words to work immediately, that is okay. Put an asterisk by all the ideas that grab you. You can go back to them and wordsmith later.

Source: Keepingithuman.com

Examples

1. An infographic aimed at getting Millennials to understand healthy food. *Caption: Why Millennials Spend Too Much on Food that Makes Them Sick, and What They Can Do About it!*

2. An eBook designed to get non-designers to create more compelling, low-cost images: *The Non-Designers No-Nonsense Guide to Kick-Ass Images Even Designers Would Envy!*

3. A blog post titled: *50 Ideas for Blog Posts That are So Fresh They Slap Themselves!*

Full disclosure: I love exclamation points because they convey excitement. I am so over quota on using them in this section!!!!!!!!!! I will stop now!!! I mean it! (Last one just for my editor).

Big Tips: Think like a journalist. What's the big takeaway that tells people 1) why they should care; 2) what they get out of your content; and 3) what is surprising, helpful, funny or unexpected.

If you are having trouble encapsulating your content into one key engaging concept, you may need to rethink your content until your framing is clear, crisp, and compelling. Don't create your content until you nail your headline because it is your lens that frames your writing or design work.

If it fries your brain a bit, that's good! That means you are building new ways of thinking. And you can have a margarita to celebrate later. You are what you eat, so by 5pm your time, you can be a margarita and chips with salsa.

Your Turn: Spend 5 Minutes Creating Captions for Your Content

Exercise 7: Forward/Reverse (or "Thinking Backwards")

Great uses: idea generation for new products, content, and customer service. I used this activity with a software-as-a-service (SaaS) company to create better customer service and fun content for their marketing. I also used this activity at a product conference and saw product peoples' eyes light up when they realized how they could use this back in their teams. And I used this with a high-tech team to come up with a bunch of new content ideas for videos. This activity works as well solo as with a team, although a team gives you more creative energy to see new things.

In improv, the game "forward/reverse" fries my brain. The results on the stage are hysterical. That is the point—to mess with the improviser so badly on stage that you fail boldly and the audience cracks up!

How it Works (in improvisation): Start a scene with a big action and the referee, a fellow improviser or an audience member (in your brainstorming team, it would be a designated team member) yells "reverse" or "forward," at any time.

When this happens, the improviser must repeat an action and/or dialogue with 'reverse' and again with 'forward' as instructed. If 'reverse,' you do it again. If forward, you repeat the information and then forward the scene beyond that point until the ref/team member shouts either a 'forward' or 'reverse' command again. You don't have to worry about that. That's the stage version.

In a brainstorming session, I put an emphasis on reversal, or thinking backwards. If I say to you or your team, "Come up with 10 ways to save money," you could likely do it. But after perhaps the third or fourth (or maybe even fifth) idea, you would likely:

- ✓ run out of ideas
- ✓ repeat stuff
- ✓ run out of steam quickly

It's hard to see fresh things in a forward motion at times because we've always done it this way. So your brain can stop seeing new things when we do things the same way all the time. And it's hard to innovate on command. "Hey team! Go over there and innovate!" What the hell does that even mean?! Ideas don't always work that way.

That is the beauty of using improv-inspired brainstorming exercises. You will look at content in ways you didn't before, so you will see new things. When you cannot see any new ideas, that is your brain's way of telling you to mix it up, do something different and try new things in order to see new opportunities.

This exercise has **TWO KEY PARTS**.

Part I: I start with all the ways we could intentionally make something worse. While sometimes ideas for making things better aren't obvious, it's pretty easy to come up with ideas for making things worse. Starting backwards is often easier.

Example

To illustrate and have fun, we'll start with a specific question: *How can we make our content worse?* **List all the possibilities:**

- ✓ Talk all about ourselves and our products
- ✓ Be really boring
- ✓ Have no sense of humor
- ✓ Talk about customers like they are companies, not people
- ✓ Repeat ourselves
- ✓ Never use images or video
- ✓ Ignore comments in social media
- ✓ Offend people with our insensitivity around social issues
- ✓ Never say what we stand for
- ✓ Don't commit to making the world better

Now there is probably a lot more you could come up with here in terms of ways to screw content up.

Part II: In this second part, go down your list from part I and ask yourself, "How can we reverse this and make it better?" So you do that for each item. Now you can see areas for improvement in each item you made worse. Going back now to our original list from Part I, we are going to reverse each *made worse* item to make it better:

✓ Talk constantly about the company and about our products. **Reverse: talk about our community and people a lot more. Feature a new community member each week.**

✓ Be really boring. **Reverse: create contests, quizzes, and interactive content. Banish boring!**

✓ Have no sense of humor. **Reverse: Make sure we have enough personality together with value so that users know we take what we do seriously, but not ourselves so seriously. Implement a weekly fun content day, where we make sure content is light-hearted. Invite users to create fun content and share.**

✓ Talk about customers like they are companies, not people. **Reverse: Feature one story per week, focusing on a specific customer (person, not company). Make them look good. (Focus on your customer as hero!)**

✓ Repeat ourselves. **Reverse: review the content calendar for ideas that are fresh and different, and provide updates on earlier stories so we have a fresh angle on an older story (serial storytelling, for example).**

✓ Never use images or video. **Reverse: Make sure at least 3 non-stock (that everyone uses) images accompany each post and that we post X number of videos per week.**

✓ Ignore comments in social media: **Reverse: take comments and make our content better and then re-release a few pieces asking our users for feedback in making them better. Or ask users to make their versions of our content and then share those. Have content awards for our users.**

✓ Offend people with our insensitivity around social issues. **Reverse: make sure we are sensitive on the topics our customers care about. Reach out to them and ask, and make it clear with our content what issues we care about. Consider a customer advisory committee.**

✓ Never say what we stand for. **Reverse: make sure our purpose story is advanced in everything we do.**

✓ Don't commit to making the world better. **Reverse: make sure we show people how our company and our customers are helping make others' lives better. Curate and share these stories. And let's feature our employees in regular videos or chats. They are the voice of our company and our best brand champions!**

By making things worse (first) and then reversing each item to make it better, we see areas and ideas we might not have considered before.

Sometimes making things better (thinking forward first) just isn't as obvious.

Another example of thinking backwards (or maybe even "upside down") that I really like is *The Human Walking Program*[xii], created by a pet adoption service in Australia. Instead of a campaign to rescue animals by having people walk dogs, they established a "human walking program," where the focus was on the idea that people need rescuing by these wonderful animals. It worked! They made dogs the clients – what a wonderful way to reverse assumptions and create a new possibility for marketing.

Your Turn: Spend at least 5 minutes generating ideas on how you could screw up your content, and then another 5 minutes going down the list and reversing those items for a total of 10 minutes.

Exercise 8: Replay

Great uses: getting unstuck, idea generation for content, product and service innovation, branding, and customer experience design. I used this activity with several clients to sharpen their brand strategies, including voice, content, and how that voice plays out on social media. Anytime you need to "replay" or try on different things to see what fits, replay is a great activity. I do it in groups much more than I do solo. I think it works optimally this way.

Replay is a game that allows you to replay a scene or an idea over with a few changes each time you *replay it*. I love playing this exercise on an improvisation stage, and I love using it to help teams. It's so much fun!

How it Works: Take an idea and create a scene or narrative around it. Now, replay that scene (works great for campaign and content ideas!) with new suggestions each time and see where it goes.

Example

I like to play this as a brand identity, content or product idea generation game. For example, assume you have an idea for a blog post: *How Managing Your SEO is like Chess*. Run through as many ideas that show how managing SEO is like chess until you can't go anymore, or go for 5 minutes, whichever comes first.

Then, replay this idea as another metaphor. Don't worry about a perfect metaphor. Perhaps this time you try: *How Managing Your SEO is like Baseball*. Run through as many ideas as you can generate in 5 minutes or until you run out of ideas.

Replay it again based on a new suggestion out of the realm of sports. You will find inspiration mixing ideas (remember mash-ups?). Maybe this time it's *How Managing Your SEO is like Baking Cookies*. Rinse and repeat the process. Don't stay in the sports metaphor world, or any world, too long. Try different things until you hit an a-ha where you have found a great metaphor that generates enough ideas to write about to support your blog post, video, campaign, or whatever with great ideas.

I usually do this with 3-5 replays. You can do more or fewer until you start generating a lot of ideas. You will know when you hit on something good because you will be able to come up with 7-10 or likely more items for your metaphor.

Your Turn: Take 5 Minutes to Replay a campaign or post idea

Exercise 9: If That is True, What Else is True?

Great uses: getting unstuck, personal development, service and product innovation, as well as content ideas. I use this one a lot when I am helping companies and their marketing teams think about their customer personas and how to go beyond that to making content based on wants and needs. This exercise helps to not only flesh out personas, but also to think about customer needs in a way that helps us understand, empathize, and develop helpful solutions. I use this activity solo and in teams.

This is a wonderful exercise that works your brain to create hypotheses about your market, your ideal customers, and their needs. It can also be used to create more fleshed-out personas; and, by doing so, help your organization understand more specifically what types of products, services, and content your customers need.

How it Works: Start with a statement about your customer that you know is true. Then ask, "If that's true, what else is true about them?" You are making best-guess statements. Don't judge yourself. It's not about intellectual accuracy. It's about allowing your brain to go to creative places by making educated assumptions that allow us to build a profile of likes, needs, and wants. And you can guess certain things that likely occur together. People who shop organic tend to care about local sourcing, health, and tend to have higher incomes, for example. Most likely, they read a lot about nutrition and care what they put in their bodies and feed to their families. These all make sense together, and they are reasonable guesses.

Example

Here is how this might play out by making a few, specific best-guess statements: Start with a fact—something you know to be true—and build on that.

Imagine your audience is 25 to 40-year-old tech professionals in the SF Bay Area. They attend many events and are socially-minded. Now we extrapolate:

✓ Our customers love networking in person and are adventurous.

- ✓ Our customers would love to meet other like-minded people in their age ranges for friendship, business, and dating.
- ✓ Our customers love experimenting with new experiences, people, and food.
- ✓ Our customers would love a home-cooked meal delivered to them where they could invite their friends.
- ✓ Our customers would love to turn this into a get-together with poetry, comedy, trying new apps and social technologies, and having a great time.
- ✓ Our customers are tech-savvy and would be willing to try new apps that take them to different peoples' houses for drinks, dinner, dessert, coffee—like a bar crawl, except this would be a *"try new food crawl."*
- ✓ Our customers would be up for trying a new in-home dining / catering app that allows them to invite their friends.
- ✓ Our customers would be open to an app that lets them go to other peoples' houses to try new foods and meet new people.

As you can see, each item builds on the previous. We accept each item as true and add on: *if this is true, what else is true?*

Go past the obvious five minutes. You will have ideas for new services you could test, for a new video, or for other content directed toward your audience. If you are an app company, how cool would be it be to offer a top five list of *Places Every Millennial Should Try*, or *How to Create an In-Home Poetry Slam?* Or consider a "food crawl" social app! You want to go past your products and services in terms of what you already offer and find new ways to create value for things in which your audience would be interested.

Your Turn: Go for 5 Minutes. You know you want to!

Exercise 10: I Like That and...

Great uses: getting unstuck, warming up, idea generation for new products, content, events, branding, and customer experience design. You can use for internal purposes, too. I use this to help teams take ideas they have honed in on and flesh them out so they see possibility. I even did this for internal communications at a pharmaceutical company that had lots of Millennial new hires and needed to bring more fun and flexibility into the work environment. A winery used it to create in-person events so regular customers could meet each other. Those events informed the type of marketing the winery started, including more meet-ups to develop community. Use this one solo or in teams. As always, teams create a powerful, creative energy that helps further idea generation.

This exercise is a lot like "Yes, and." You are building sequentially onto ideas others have offered before you.

How it Works: Someone will say an idea. Each subsequent person will say, "I like that and...(add onto it). You can go for at least 5 minutes until you get some pretty crazy ideas. By validating what you like, other ideas you like will pop up for you.

See the Exercise details for the "Yes, and" Exercise 2, in this section. The same "how it works" details apply here.

Your Turn: Go for at least 5 minutes!

Exercises 11 and 12: Status Shifts and Role Reversals

Great uses: idea generation for stories, video campaigns, all kinds of great content. I have even used this for my business, as well as for clients. I sat down with a group of kids and had them talk about jargon and why adults are bad at clear communication. The results were hilarious[xiii]. I also used these techniques with a few nonprofits needing to tell their stories in more engaging ways. After I presented at a conference last year, I gave some advice to a tech company. They then used kids to read their parents' resumes out loud and created a video around it. Brainstorm solo or in teams here.

Two of my favorite storytelling techniques from improvisation (and we talked about this in a prior chapter) include status shifts and role reversals. These techniques are great ways to flip expectations upside down. That's the whole point of this chapter (and book). When you flip content, you change the way you see things. That is when the a-ha hits you in the face (with love, of course!). And boring will be a bad memory.

I am using status shifts and role reversals together because they often (though not always) occur together and can be used in tandem.

How it Works: Status shifts are narrative arc changes that occur when characters switch status. High-status characters become low-status characters and vice-versa.

Here are some ways status shifts could play out:

- ✓ The unethical millionaire banker gets caught, goes to prison and becomes the prison janitor
- ✓ The new immigrant who speaks little English saves the day and becomes a hero when he resuscitates a child pulled from the water
- ✓ The poorly educated, good and kind-hearted salt of the earth couple hit the lottery and become millionaires who donate to charity and help people
- ✓ The hot-shot programmer genius who treats people poorly gets fired

There are so many scenarios that can happen. Status shifts speak to our desire for justice and comeuppance, and for an equitable and emotionally satisfying resolution (and change in the status quo) in a story. And, as I will demonstrate momentarily, they can be used for content ideas, too, because they turn our assumptions upside-down.

Role Reversals are a bit similar, though they need not come with a switch in status; for example a husband and wife switch roles. Or business partners switch roles, for example. This *can* be part of a status shift certainly. So, for instance, if the janitor and CEO switch roles for a day, then that is both a status shift and role reversal. Suppose a child and parent switch behaviors – that, too, is both a role reversal and status shift.

Source: gratisography.com

So let's explore!

Example

Imagine these fun scenarios for creative, fun, engaging content:

✓ You're a tech company that knows it has too much jargon. Video a bunch of kids and ask them what your company does and to explain in it in *their* words. Kids are brilliant and they will find ways to call BS on your BS! The results can be fun, fresh, and hysterical because they will use their words and it will make more sense. I did this for my business.

✓ Have your employees' kids read their parents' job descriptions and video it. Again, the results will be fun. Ask them in their words what their parents do for a living! (LinkedIn did this and it was pretty funny!)

✓ Channeling *Undercover Boss*, have your boss switch places with a newly hired employee and record what happens for a few hours. What would that look like? It would likely be funny, enlightening, and humbling. Use some of these clips as videos for social media to highlight empathy and a lighter, human touch. And to show your customers that your boss gets it and that you value humility, humor and feedback.

✓ Invite a few key customers to a brainstorming meeting and ask them what marketing they would create and what products they might innovate. Video it and use that video for your marketing, or just use the ideas they come up with in your content.

✓ Ask a select group of customers to run your company for a meeting. Record the meeting. There will undoubtedly be great ideas you can use.

✓ Ask your customers (video) what they think your company does. Cisco did this with 'cloud-computing' and asked people at a conference to explain what that term meant. The results were pretty funny, as you can imagine. I mean who outside of tech people really understands "cloud computing?" And even many tech people don't really understand it.

✓ Take your content and have a customer edit it or create their 'new and improved' version of it. Post the results.

✓ Take a story that is not finished yet and ask your customers to write their version of the ending.

✓ Have your CEO interview an employee and record it or vice-versa.

✓ Have your CEO interview himself/herself (through the magic of editing. Several years ago, SAP's CEO Hasso Plattner did this, and it was highly amusing!)

There are so many ways to use status shifts and role reversals to create great content. When people switch things up, the unexpected happens, and that is a beautiful, un-boring thing!

Your Turn: Spend 10 Minutes on this.

Exercise 13: A Day in the Life

Great uses: idea generation for stories, video campaigns, all kinds of great content and branding. This is a great exercise to hone your branding voice and ask yourself, "What content could we produce with this voice that is fun and compelling?" "As a personality, who is our brand?" This exercise is ideally suited for team development.

A Day in the Life is another short-form game (5 minutes or less) on stage.

How it Works (in improvisation): Improvisers will ask for an audience volunteer. That volunteer will come onstage and be interviewed about his or her day. They will be asked about their friends, how their day started, what big events happened that day, and anything distinct about that day's happenings. The volunteer's friends and family will also supply a few key words to describe the audience volunteer's personality!

Then, improvisers will act this out on a stage and take it way over the top. That means a lot of exaggeration. That's where the fun is.

How this Works (for your idea generation): Imagine your brand is a person. Because it is! What are its attributes? It could be funny, helpful, dependable, luxurious, and insightful to name a few. Be specific about those attributes up front. You should already know your brand personality. This exercise can sharpen that saw, and help you see instances where your brand voice needs clarity.

Have someone on your team play the role of your brand as a person with those attributes. Have a few people interview him or her or just have a casual conversation. Ask questions about your services, about your customers, about your marketing, about what passions your users have. Have your 'brand personality' answer them. Give your brand a name that fits based on your company values, passions, whatever. Record it.

Where does your brand hit the nail on the head? Where does it go off-topic? Where does it make you laugh? What does your brand think of all the things your customer cares about? Imagine your brand has a lot to say about mobile apps. What advice would it give customers? Imagine it's a Q&A with your customers.

Imagine these conversations and answers are content pieces or blog-posts you create for users. You could try an "ask our brand anything" day and publish the responses (as your brand would answer them) across your social media channels.

Make it a regular thing if it works. Test it and run with it several times per month. You can do this as a text chat and a live video stream, too. "Ask our brand anything" days would be a great way to experiment, humanize your brand, and do something fresh that adds value for your audience, and allow you to have some fun, too. When you have more fun, your audience does.

Your Turn: 10 Minutes

✓ What is your brand personality?
✓ What would your brand do every day as a person?
✓ What advice would your brand give in a chat with users?
✓ Role-play this with your team! Imagine a conversation between your brand and ideal users. What would that conversation sound like?

Exercise 14: What Happens Next?

Great uses: warming up, content, and storytelling. I have used this for content ideas and to help marketing teams work on their own company stories to get to the stuff that matters —that human layer! It's great to do this exercise solo when you are working on your own things, but also great to use in teams.

Remember Chapter Two's Story Spine? Well, the middle section of that model is a great device for advancing and fleshing out a story idea beyond the spine, and I use it for this exact purpose. The part I am referring to:

Because of that...
Because of that...
Because of that...

A great story or content idea answers the question *then what?* This section forces us to answer *what comes next?* Remember when you were little and you asked your parents "what happens next?" as they read stories to you? This doesn't stop when we become adults! Our brains want action and consequences. We crave that narrative detail in our stories.

How it Works: So when you are thinking about your content or story, answer the 'what comes next?' or 'so what?' for your audience. What does X enable people to do? And because of that, what does Y enable them to do? And because of that, what does Z enable them to do?

You keep pulling back layers of the onion until you get to the heart of your human story. This was an exercise we used in chapter two.

This exercise forces you to further develop your stories. As you do that, you will also uncover more ideas for stories and content than you expected. Each "this happens next" could even be a separate story in a serial storytelling effort.

Once you have that human story, you can create follow-up stories, side stories, related stories, customer stories about how their human needs were met, or have your customers develop content about their experiences with your products and services (think: GoPro) and share it!

Your Turn: Spend 10 Minutes Asking "What Happens Next?" in a few of your stories.

Exercise 15: Clash of Contexts / Fish Out of Water

Great uses: idea generation for stories and for fun and funny content. Clash of contexts and contrast is what amplifies the funny. I use this technique for my content, and I did a content session with a large, high-tech company recently where a lot of great ideas were generated. Use this exercise for content, stories, and sketches (I use it for my writing and comedy sketches). This one is a staple in my comedy arsenal. My life is a fish out of water story! Use this activity solo or as a team. Either way, you will get great results.

Source: gratisography.com

This technique is used in comedy writing all the time, and I've written about it extensively over the years in blog posts and eBooks. I use this technique for my own work and with clients. Clash of contexts uses incongruity and juxtaposition to highlight comedy. The "fish out of water" idea is a staple for sitcoms and movies: *Kindergarten Cop, Meet the Parents, Beverly Hills Cop*, and so many more.

How it Works: Put the main character in a world he or she is not used to and see how that person adapts. How does everyone around that person adapt? That clash of contexts, of people from different worlds, highlights the incongruous. And taking the contrast over the top (through exaggeration) is a way to heighten the comedy. It is this big contrast of worlds that makes creative, funny, and fresh content!

Source: Keepingithuman.com

Examples

Imagine a portable GPS with an identity crisis in the wake of mobile apps that render it obsolete. Put this GPS in a therapy group. What would it say? Or maybe it goes to an unemployment office to try to adapt and get a new job? Another great demonstration of comical contrasts is the Sprint commercial featuring actors Malcolm McDowell and James Earl Jones reading texts written by teens. Here are two very well known, award-winning actors doing dramatic readings of texts sent by teenage girls with a penchant for, well, teen-isms: "OMG. Adorbs," and, "Totally

Hottie McHotterson," for example. It's a funny contrast.

What would your product or service say in completely absurd situations? What if you changed the historical context for your product and put in it in the past or the future?

- ✓ A caveman would do what with your product or service?
- ✓ What would a robot do?
- ✓ How about a drone?
- ✓ What if the family of the future found your product or service? What would they do with it?

Think how people would react to this change of context. What would be funny in the way they relate to the product/service? What would they do/think/feel about it?

Maybe send an employee to the future or past to talk about the product. Would people in the Renaissance have their own jargon? Probably. How funny would that conversation be—the clash of jargon contexts?!

As another example, what would have been the closest thing people during the American Revolution would have had to a ride-sharing service? Would it be a horse-drawn carriage or a guy on a horse with a bugle, shouting, "Hey, your horse is here!" Show how ride-sharing has evolved through the ages in your campaign. Put a modern app in the past and show that clash of contexts. That is a fun way to show evolution in your product. Imagine that on video, in images, or in an infographic: the evolution of ride-sharing.

Your Turn: Take 10 Minutes and Put Your Product/Service into Different Contexts

Exercise 16: 50 Titles in 5 Minutes or Less

Great uses: rapid-fire idea generation for just about anything. I have used it for products and services ideas, and I use it all the time for content article titles. Most recently, I did a round of this with a nonprofit. We generated 50 ideas. The company is currently working 20 of these ideas into its editorial calendar. I love when that happens. I use this activity all the time for my own idea generation. I even did it with a few friends and mentors when I was generating ideas for the title of this book! Do this activity by yourself or as part of a team.

How it works: In this exercise, the goal is to not overthink things too much. We slow down idea generation when we judge the ideas as we're moving along. This exercise asks you and / or your team to brainstorm article ideas or titles - 50 of them – in 5 minutes or less.

Your first ideas might feel redundant or boring…or just not inspiring. The first two-thirds of ideas most teams generate are obvious. Most teams stop after reaching this point. But the true gems are often found when you push past the upper two-thirds and get to what is creatively called *the lower third*. This section is when you start generating ideas that are fresh, exciting, and fun. Your brain needs the warm-up time to get in flow.

Example

Suppose the goal (and be specific) is to generate 50 article titles on how to create better content. That's a pretty boring how-to and generic concept. So let's start brainstorming and list as many ideas as we can (before you read my list which I wrote in 5 minutes, try brainstorming your own ideas on this topic). It doesn't have to be 50 ideas. Go for *at least* 25. Under that isn't enough for your brain to kick into high creative gear. The more you do, the faster your brain will work. It gets on a roll and you'll get more ideas and better ones as you go!

Here we go (a number of Post Titles):

1. *Channeling Your Content Guide: Lessons From the Golden State Warriors*

2. *Lessons on Creating Great Content From my Dog, Buddy (note: my Dog's name is Buddy! Substitute your dog's name!)*

3. *Why Creating Great Content is a Lot Like Parenting*

4. *Everything I learned about Creating Compelling Content I Learned From Reality TV (note: I don't actually watch it! You can substitute your own show here).*

5. *Why I Failed at Content the First Few Years and What I Learned From It*

6. *Great Content is Over-rated and Here's Why*

7. *When Content Fails Blame Your Stories*

8. *Life Lessons about Business and Great Content from the Basketball Court*

9. *Creating Content the Michael Jordan Way*

10. *Kicking Ass and Taking Content Names The Stephan Curry Way*

11. *What Key and Peele Can Teach Marketers about "Nooice" Content (side note: I already wrote this post because I love Key and Peele[xiv]. Did I mention I am a comedy nerd?)*

12. *How to Uberize Your Content – What Ride Sharing Taught Me about Life*

13. *How Most Content Plans are Bullshit and What You Can Do*

14. *Observations on Contagious Content from a Stand-Up Comic (note: I wrote this already on John Oliver)[xv]*

15. *What do Shark Tank, The Walking Dead, and Brooklyn 99 have in common?*

16. *Your Content is Killing Me and Here's What to Do About It*

17. *I Threw My Content Calendar out the Window and Why You Should, Too*

18. *The Content Apocalypse is Coming, and It's Scarier Than You Think*

19. *What Your Grandpa knows about Stories That Would Change Your Life*

20. *How to Create Inspiring Content Without Sounding Like a Jerk*

21. *I Switched Places with my Husband for a Day of Work. Here's What Happened*

22. *My Kid Re-wrote my Content Plan and Made it Better*

23. *Why Your First Content Instincts are Wrong*

24. *How to Help People Be Better – It's Not What You Think*

25. *What Happened to Brand Journalism and Why You Should Care*

26. *How I Generated Ten Content Pieces from a 10-Minute Periscope and You Can, Too*

27. *How My First F in School Taught Me Everything About Content Creation*

28. *Why You Should Ignore the Content Experts*

29. *Why The Onion is the Only Content Source You Need for Inspiration*

30. *A Funny Thing Happened on the Way to the Content Marketing Conference*

31. *How a Content Nightmare Helped Me Unlearn Bad Habits*

32. *Content, Humor, and Life Lessons From The Muppets*

33. *How My Dad's Hatred for My Writing Made it Better*

34. *Inspirational Quotes from Authors to Help Ignite Your Creativity*

35. *My Grandma Thinks 'Content Marketing' is a Made-Up Profession. Here's Where She's Right.*

36. *Why the Eighth Layer in Dante's Inferno is Filled with Content Marketers!*

Whew! I promised 50....let's keep going....

37. *Don't Point Your Content at Me!*

38. *Your Content Underwear is Showing*

39. *Content Lessons From an Unrepentant Grammar Snob*

40. *What Coming In Last at Kickball Taught Me About Kick-Ass Content*

41. *If I Had Wanted a Nap, I Would Read Your Content*

42. *Why Kick-Ass Content is the New Black*

43. *The Worst Thing to Happen to Content Marketing is The Rise of The Content Marketer*

44. *Bottle It! How to Tell Stories That Work Every Time*

45. *Your Content Wouldn't Pass The First-Grader Sniff Test, and What You Can Learn From a 7-Year-Old*

46. *My Content Team Can Beat Up Your Content Team*

47. *Monty Python, Comedy, and One Woman's Search For the Holy Content Grail*

48. *Your Pet Wants to Murder You in Your Sleep (note: not Content related per se, but it made me laugh!)*

49. *Content, Your Voice, and One Big Lesson Susan Boyle (substitute someone you like here) Taught Me About Standing Out*

50. *The Hitchhiker's Guide to the Content Marketing Universe+1: Because Great Lessons Don't Always End with 42!*

As with any methodology, these ideas are not all equally viable. Some are funny and would surely stand out. The key is to go nuts and write down as many things as you can without stopping. As you push past the obvious ideas, it might take you a few minutes to get to that next level of creativity. You'll notice you might not hit anything for a short time. Once you do, however, the floodgates open and you'll have more ideas as one idea leads to the next and the next…and on you go. The less you judge your ideas and just write, the more ideas you will generate.

The above list is my list. What will **you** do?

Your Turn. Do at least 25 titles in 5 minutes! If you can do 50, that's even better. Start with one title and go from there.

Exercise 17: I Kissed a...

Great uses: warming up, mind-mapping, and generating content ideas. It's a fabulous word association game, so you can generate all kinds of fun stuff—from video campaign ideas to blog posts to images and visual storytelling fun. This activity is a great way to explore. I use it alone and in teams.

How it Works: This is a pun-based game. Take any word or object and create a pun-based joke from it. It gets you onto a creative mode, and you can springboard into idea generation from there.

You: I kissed an 'X object' (substitute whatever you like for X)
Your team asks: What did you get?
You: PUNchline (see what I did there?)

Example

Suppose your word is *pen*. Now, following the format above...

"I kissed a pen..."

Your Team: "What did you get?"

"Kicked in the ball-point!"

"I kissed a pen..."

Your Team: "What did you get?"

"I won't Teller."

_*"I kissed a pen."*

Your Team: "What did you get?"

"A lot of BICkering."

This is improv's approach to mind-mapping on a whiteboard. Start with a word that you want to create content around. Another example might be "apps." See if anything comes up that could be further explored as an idea for content.

"I kissed an app."

Your Team: "What did you get?"

"It wasn't in person. iPhoned it in."

"I kissed an app."
Your Team: "What you get?"

"Appoplectic."

"I kissed an app."

Your Team: "What did you get?"

"SLAPPed!"

You can use this game to come up with a top 5 (or top X) made-up iPhone apps for your audience as a post (these could be "what if" apps related to the word you used to start with!). That could be a great post, campaign, video or infographic. Or maybe a 'top X list' post of puns based off of your product's name (Top Names We Didn't Pick!). If you poke fun at yourself and use a little levity, your audience will love it.

Your Turn: Try Doing this with a Few Key Words For Your Business. Go for 5 Minutes.

Exercise 18: Stream of Consciousness

Great uses: for anything, really. Use to get unstuck and come up with product and service ideas, content ideas, and customer service ideas...you name it. I do this mostly alone but sometimes with teams. I did this exercise among others when brainstorming for the name of this book.

How it Works: Write it out or go Motor-Mouth style and talk it out. Even better, mind map all the ideas (draw out ideas and connect them to each other as you come up with related ideas) that come to you as you talk. Sounds hard? It really isn't. There is no right or wrong. The first two minutes may feel weird. Thereafter, you will unearth all kinds of ideas. Be specific about a challenge because that helps. One example for framing it tightly could be: *how can I make an article more interesting?* Or *how can I generate 10 titles in 5 minutes?* Or *how can I create more content around how to recycle wire hangers?*

Your Turn: Try it for 10 minutes.

Exercise 19: What Are You Doing?

There are several ways to play this game. To make it easy, I like to go to the more challenging prompts. Use it to generate ideas for content, for warm-up or for getting un-stuck. We get stuck because we overthink things. When you stop overthinking things, you will make "mistakes." They really aren't mistakes in the true creative sense. That's good news — that means your brain is going fast. You will also generate some pretty funny ideas this way. Notice that the biggest laughs come from not being perfect or getting everything "right." Related? Absolutely!

You can do this alone (answer for your partner) or in small teams (best in a team of two or three).

How it Works: Get a suggestion for an activity. One person starts doing something—anything. Then, after a few seconds, another person asks the person doing the action, "what are you doing?" They then have to give a suggestion for the other person to act out (not say what they are doing – only a new activity for someone else to act out).

So, if the suggestion for everyone is ABC, the person that went first uses each letter in the suggestion to answer the question of what they are doing. For ABC, one answer is "**A**rticulating **B**inary **C**odes," and that becomes what the next person must act out with some verbal component. Then, you ask that person what he/she is doing. That person must say something new (as a suggestion to the next person): **A**mplifying **B**ellicose **C**reatures (the next person acts that out). Keep going until someone's brain fries and then you get a new acronym suggestion, such as "CAD." Every "what are you doing?" must then be answered with words that match that acronym: **C**atching **A**lligator **D**ogma!

Besides frying your brain and making you laugh, this particular exercise frees up your creative juices and gets you over the stuck-in-a-rut syndrome. From there, you can move on to another exercise.

Your Turn: Try it for 10 minutes.

Exercise 20: Motivational Poster

Great uses: idea generation for stories, images and videos, and for fun and funny content. I use this for visual storytelling with clients and for blog post and image ideas for my business. This started out as a game my improvisation group invented. The game worked well in practice, so we tried it in a show. The result made the audience and all of us crack up as we did it, so we thought why the heck not? Let's keep using it! It works solo or in teams. However, because creative energy sparks when others are involved, that's where it gets the most juice.

One of my new favorite games that my improvisation group and I came up with is motivational poster. You know those cheesy office posters with the motivational slogans on them? Example: that famous cat poster with the caption, "Hang in there"? That's the point of this exercise: to come up with fun ideas that could be the basis for new content.

How it Works: Use targeted words related to your business or random words. I suggest starting with buzzwords because they are easy to poke fun of.

KATHY KLOTZ-GUEST

Funny Food for Thought....What's **an Infocrapic?**

Infocrapic. -Noun. Def:

An infographic made crappy by cramming too many unimportant facts into a single picture. Also, readability is made worse with small font size and too many headings.

Sentence usage: "Stop creating *infocrapics.* (pl.)"

Source: Keepingithuman.com

Example

One example might be "disruption."

For the word "disruption," generate as many poster captions as you can:

"When normal words just aren't enough."

"When you're not afraid of getting smacked for jargon."

"When you're all out of buzzwords."

"Because paradigm-shifts are so 2007."

"Because we've already used 'game-changing' 100 times.

"Nothing says nothing like 'disruption.'"

"When yesterday's jargon won't do."

"A fancy way of saying 'we don't know what the hell else to say.'"

Your Turn: Spend 5 minutes coming up with motivational posters (one snappy phrase) for a word. Start with a word you dislike or a word that your organization over-uses and that you all agree you don't like. Have fun with it.

Exercise 21: Motivational Poster with Irony (Now, fortified with extra Iron-y!)

Great uses: idea generation for stories, for images and videos, and for fun and funny content. I often use this for visual storytelling with clients and I also use it for blog post and image ideas for my business. I love using this one for images, especially! And it can be used alone or in small groups.

Directions are just like Motivation Poster above (Exercise 20) with the following modification: When you get your captions done...to add irony, take your caption and write the opposite. *So if we take a few from the prior exercise, we have:*

"When normal words just aren't enough."

Opposite: Normal words say everything right.

"When you're not afraid of getting smacked for jargon."

Opposite: When you are scared of buzzwords.

"When you're all out of buzzwords."

Opposite: When you have buzzwords coming out your buzzword pie hole for days. (Note: buzzword pie hole makes me laugh!)

Any of the above could make very funny images, infographics, and/or titles for posts. You could also turn this caption idea into a user contest and then ask your audience to share their creations. People love to share content they created.

Your Turn: Try a few words and go for 5 Minutes

Chapter Nine Summary

The activities I have outlined are some of my favorites. There are dozens more that I didn't outline in this book. And I am creating my own and adapting new exercises all the time. You can make your own activities, too. The big thing is, to create differently you need to see things differently. So incorporate a few of these into your regular brainstorming and you'll notice the difference in creative energy and output. And boring won't be a problem!

If you still get stuck, call me. I help companies with storytelling and content and uncovering new ideas, and I love facilitating by bringing my improvisation comedy and marketing backgrounds together. And I use all of these activities and more in my work. I also help companies design their own exercises, so they can use them anytime they get stuck and for a variety of needs beyond marketing and storytelling.

Next Up...

By now you're probably thinking, "*Wow, that's a lot of stuff!*" It is.

I hope you will use some of these exercises sooner rather than later so you can start putting those amazing, creative ideas of yours to work. Remember, not everything will be viable. This is true, regardless of whatever methodology you use to generate new ideas. You will be surprised, however, at how many ideas are doable. And you can use these exercises for so many things beyond marketing and content.

We're almost done. Way to go. Next up, in the last chapter, I leave you with some closing thoughts on how to document results so you can go back to what works.

Name three activities you will try this week:

_____

_____

Your favorite exercise is:

_____

_____

You have questions about:

_____

_____

After reading this section, you have the following ideas (list all):

_____

_____

_____

_____

_____

_____

_____

_____

_____

Source: Keepingithuman.com

10
FINAL THOUGHTS: SAFE IS RISKY

We covered a lot of ground, and it's a lot to take in. You did it! The good news is that you don't have to implement these ideas all at once. Just start somewhere. Anywhere. Make that creative commitment to yourself and to your team. You have so much to unleash. I am excited for you, your team, and your prospects and customers. Don't forget to let me know how it goes.

I have a few final thoughts to help you get the most out of these exercises.

Safe is Risky

If you have gotten this far in the book, you probably have more questions. Whether it's having humorous content or just creating bolder content without the funny, you might be wondering how to manage risk. Some of the ideas you generate may feel riskier than others, especially if you work in conservative industries. I get it. I came out of high-tech, and it wasn't always progressive, light-hearted or willing to try new things. Some companies had a very conservative outlook.

Based on my experiences, here are a few thoughts:

First truth: you won't please everyone. No matter what you do. I know this first-hand.

Second truth: all innovation comes with some risk. That's life. Do you want to be comfortable or do you want to create something remarkable? As with investing: no risk, no reward.

Third truth: if you come up with ideas that you think might push the envelope for your organization, test them with a small group of people. Testing them with a large group tends to kill creativity because risk-aversion is contagious. There is no great creativity by committee;

however, there is death by committee! It's often easier to get support from a few inside champions and outside ones (a key partner or top customer, for example).

Here are a few ways to think about testing small before you scale and put time and money into creating content around the ideas you generate:

- ✓ Test ideas with a small group of customers and employees outside of marketing (those closest to the customer, like sales and service, are great starting points)
- ✓ Do a small-scale split test with an idea to get quick feedback
- ✓ If you get positive feedback, then scale and spend money and time creating content
- ✓ Recruit internal (and external if possible and appropriate) champions to help you get support for the ideas
- ✓ Start with small things that feel low-risk. For example, start with a few images and see how they do before creating video. Or start with a video concept and storyboard (maybe even a rough cut of video) and get buy-in before you spend resources. Find out if there are hidden risks (legal, etc.) you don't know about other than just taking a creative risk. Risk is part of the process if you want to break the boring cycle. However, as I explain, take small risks to start.

Follow the Fear

Joseph Campbell says, "The cave you fear holds the treasure you seek." We're afraid to go into the cave. In improvisation, we have a saying: follow the fear. Move toward what scares you. I know this feeling and it happens to all of us. Even me because I won't turn in my human card! Some of this may seem a bit new and, therefore, intimidating. That's okay. Sometimes new stuff feels like that. It does sometimes for me, too. Improvisation has taught me to embrace it and know that it will be okay.

Source: Kathy Klotz-Guest

Source: Kathy Klotz-Guest. It's a poster hanging at the D-School (design school) at Stanford University.

It helps to see innovating kick-ass, bold marketing content as creative play, because it is. And you don't have to commit to ideas you generate. However, I do hope that you act on the big ones that are viable. It's time to kick "safe" and "boring" in the pants: with idea orgasms!

Now I turn to some practical advice on documenting. Ooooh. I know what you are thinking—the sexy part of this book! To that I say, "is there a non-sexy part to this book?!"

Document Results

I recommend recording (or at least writing down results immediately after) your creative sessions. Video is great. Audio alone works, if that's all you can do (in addition to creating some mind-maps) so you can go back and review your results—what worked, what needs refinement, what you noticed about times things worked or times your group stalled and why you got stuck. If you have someone on your team who can draw and create a visual recording, that's awesome, though not needed.
Note what activities you like best and what resonates most for you. Some activities will just feel fun and "in flow" for you over others. That is typical. While I love all of these activities, I tend to gravitate toward certain ones, depending on the situation. All these activities help with different things, certainly. And if one doesn't work for you, another will.

I document which activities get which results (yeah, I am a nerd). It helps me know which activities to use for best results in different situations. And when I work with clients, I want them to know which activities generated which results, so they can go back to them.

One word of caution: it's tempting to use the same activities over and over. You can and will get results with these exercises no matter how many times you use them because your challenges will be different and your team members (and, thus the creative dynamics) in every session will typically change. That is the good news.

But it's important to try different activities when you are stuck and even when you aren't. So when you are no longer getting results or you just aren't feeling one activity, try a different approach. If one exercise isn't getting you where you want to go, another will. You can never have too much creative fun and inspiration. Remember, you can do these alone or in groups. And you can iterate your own versions of these games. Just get started anywhere, somewhere. And have fun.

You deserve a big hug for finishing. I can't do that in person. So this acknowledgment is your virtual high-five. Now go buy yourself something nice, other than this book, of course.

Your customer is saying, "Stop boring me!" because he or she is on overload. We all are. And I passionately believe with a healthy dose of fun and creativity, and empathy, you can create kick-ass, engaging content that gets results.

Here's to your creative and marketing success!

Source: Kathy Klotz-Guest / Keepingithuman.com

11
BONUS CHAPTER: WE'RE ALL IMPROVISERS

In 2012, NPR called Bill Clinton "The Improviser-in-Chief" [xvi] for his ability to connect with audiences by ditching the script and going off-the-cuff.

At the August 2012 Democratic Convention, Clinton brought a speech he had prepared. Yes, he prepared extensively. What he *delivered* at the event looked very different. NPR compared his prepared speech with his delivered address, and found that he improvised over half of his words at the convention. Bill Clinton is a communication master with the ability to *feel* an audience in order to connect with them more meaningfully.

This is such a powerful lesson in leadership, communication, and it's important for anyone who wants to grow in his or her career by being a better connector. When what you plan no longer fits the need at hand, great communicators and leaders are ready to ditch the script and talk to audiences in the moment where people are at - rather than shove some scripted agenda at them.

Clinton was able to sense that things had shifted and he knew he had to adapt to connect more powerfully in the moment. He talked about Obama's credibility and he told personal stories about people he had met (and he named them!) whose lives had been changed because of the work Obama's team had done on issues such as healthcare reform. People wanted hope and an emotional connection, not a speech.

Being able to tell stories to connect with people emotionally, not just intellectually, is profound. Knowing when to let go of your plans in order to embrace and adjust to changes is transformational.

Source: gratisography.com

We Improvise All the Time in Business

Improvising goes far beyond speaking. We're all improvisers. When I recently asked a group of business people I was speaking with about improvising in their daily lives, they looked like they had no idea what I was saying (I'm used to it – my family looks at me the same way!). Then I asked them to raise their hands if they often have to ditch the script, change plans quickly, listen intently, co-create with customers and co-workers, make others look good, and intuit when and how to change their approaches. At this question, every hand shot up. That's my point: We are all improvisers who have to adapt every day.

Everyone has this ability, not just great leaders. And it starts when we're young. We know how to do it – even if, sadly, some of this is squeezed out of us in adulthood. It's not the purview of the "special." Sure, we think, people like Bill Clinton are magical creatures not from this world! We're all built this way and learning to listen to that voice that says, "it's time" is a muscle that increases the more we use it.

Adaptable leaders are facile in knowing when to drop the script with speaking, with campaigns, with products, with teams and people, and they know when to change directions with content calendars, business models, and even strategic direction. They know when to change the course of their businesses and they know it because they are both prepared and they sense it. Improvisation is not the same as improvised or 'winging it.' Yes, we sometimes need to improvise in the moment; yet the principles of improvisation are about discipline. We can improvise because we are experienced, prepared (yes data matters), and we also choose to trust our instincts.

Creativity Needs Adaptable Leaders

CMO.com recently stated that 2016 is the year creativity and fearless marketing is making a comeback.[xvii] If this is the year boldness and opportunity converge, the future belongs to those who plan, take creative risks, know when to let go, and do it for the right reasons.

According to the IBM 2010 Global CEO Study, the ability to embody creative leadership is among the most important attributes for navigating and succeeding in a world of increased complexity. The study also revealed that there is a shortage of flexible, creative leaders in top companies. That's a big issue for managing the next wave of marketing and business change.

So what's a marketer to do? The answer is to create a playbook and be ready to ditch it and improvise as needed.

Source: www.wikimedia.org commons license

Common Traits of Leaders Who Ditch the Script

In talking to a number of people for this chapter, a few key traits emerge consistently when we look at these "improvisational business masters."

People who are facile in ditching the script do all of the following:

- Prepare, do research, then know when to let go
- Remain unmarried to specific outcomes
- Always give their best and move on when things don't work out
- Experiment and take risks to grow, learn and be better
- Stay connected to their gut and to others
- Exhibit vulnerability as needed
- Don't let ego get in the way (they are not invested in being right)
- Readily admit mistakes, rather than blame

Stories to Inspire Your Inner Improvisational Leader

Here are a few stories from wonderful entrepreneurs I interviewed. They inspired me, and I hope they inspire your inner improvisational leader, too.

If You Get a Feeling, Listen to It. One Step at a Time – Jess Ostroff, CEO of Don't Panic Management

After graduating college, most of my friends and colleagues were going to work for big accounting firm and investment banks. This made a lot of sense given our newly acquired business degrees, and the fact that we lived in one of the money capitals of the world, New York City. I decided to turn the opposite direction, applied for an AmeriCorps program, and hopped a flight to Los Angeles to teach math and science to underprivileged youth in one of the poorest neighborhoods in the city. It was hands-down the most difficult but rewarding experiences of my life, and seeing the difference that one person could make got me interested in spending more time in a non-profit environment. Unfortunately, I encountered so much red tape, arbitrary hierarchy, and tough management styles that I decided to look into other directions. I had joined Twitter, followed about five people, including the New York Times, and landed my first freelance client through a tweet from Jay Baer.

Being young and ambitious was a virtue, because as soon as I had enough freelance virtual assistant work, I quit my job in Los Angeles and drove up to San Francisco to celebrate. It felt big and wild and scary… but it also felt right. Flash forward to six months later, and I was starting to take on more work than I could handle. I knew there was something more that was possible there; I knew there might just be a viable business bubbling beneath the surface.

I had this overwhelming feeling that I needed to respond to this calling. I need to take my little freelance operation to the next level… but I needed to minimize distractions in order to do so. Living in Venice Beach was just too fun and frankly, the work ethic in southern California at that time was not on par with the environment I knew I needed to succeed. I decided, somewhat abruptly, to pack up my Toyota Yaris with everything I needed and to sell or give away the rest. I drove from LA to Fort Lauderdale, Florida by myself, seeing friends, making memories, and picking up free Wi-Fi wherever I could. (Fun fact: Starbucks and McDonald's were great side-of-the-road Wi-Fi options in 2010 and still are today!)

It wasn't an easy ride, and I took about 3 weeks to make the trip. I had no smartphone, just my iPod, and I stayed in crappy hotels along the way. It snowed when I was in Texas (what the heck?) and the dog I had grown up with sadly passed away. These were all obstacles, but didn't stop me from being excited and motivated once I finally made it to Florida.

I quickly got started on building my network. From Twitter chats to Facebook groups, social media clubs to Millennial meet-ups, I found that relationships were the core of my business. And investing the time and energy in building those relationships was going to be what helped me grow my business from 1 solo freelancer in 2010 to 20 Don't Panic Management team members in 2016. Today, many of the folks I talked to online back in 2010 are trusted friends and colleagues. We catch up with each other at events around the world and we refer business to each other all the time.

It's easy to get overwhelmed if you think about all the things at once. Had I worried about how I would make enough money over the lifetime of the business, where I would live, or how I would make friends, I probably wouldn't have made the leap. Instead, my biggest lesson was to listen to my gut and force myself to focus on one thing at a time. I knew I had family to fall back on if I needed help financially. I knew I had other skills I could explore if the business fell flat on its head. So, taking it one step at a time was the best thing I could do to avoid being paralyzed by fear, which is a common issue that everyone faces when trying to make a change.

If you get a feeling, listen to it. Make a plan with actionable steps. Don't agonize over all the potential negative outcomes. Put one foot in front of the other and make it happen!

Make Plans and Be Ready to Abandon Them
– Amy Harrison, Founder of HarrisonAmy Copywriting

Since heading out and working for myself back in 2008 my path of work has evolved many times. Initially it went from seeing if people would pay me enough to write for a living (they would), then would people pay me to write things I actually enjoyed (yes again), and from there into training business owners and employees how to do what I do.

I loved the training side. For years I travelled throughout Europe, to London, Sweden, Bulgaria, Spain, France, Romania and more to run copywriting workshops. The work was rewarding and with every session I learned something new about presenting the materials in a new way to make it easier for people to understand.

I decided one year that corporate training was the only thing I wanted to do. It was lucrative, and so I put hours and hours into creating a strategy and marketing materials to crack the corporate market and promote my workshops. On paper it was a solid, sensible idea.

Until one day I had a workshop experience so horrible and uncomfortable it made me scrap everything I'd been working on. The people didn't want to be there, the abilities were mixed from beginner to expert so just as I was getting through to some I was losing others. Technical hitches, breakdowns in communication. It was a nightmare. And it was a huge blow. I'd spent months gearing up my business this way and then realized I didn't actually like pursuing this work. I didn't enjoy the back and forth, the company politics, the battle to encourage change. In my early days of training, companies approached me because someone knew my work, were open and keen to change and wanted to learn what I could teach.

I knew the material worked. I knew businesses could transform their corporate writing. But it was time-intensive and when half the battle is convincing someone you're needed, it's exhausting. I wanted to find a hungry crowd that I could reach in the hundreds and thousands. I scrapped the corporate training site and after much soul-searching put everything online in a brand new membership site for people who wanted access to copywriting training materials: Write With Influence.

It was a big change, but I learned that even when you realize the path you're on is one you want to abandon, the steps that got you there can still be used. I still had my ability to teach and I had solid materials ready-to-use. All I needed to do was find a way to deliver this in a way that made me and my customers happy. My big lesson: make plans and be ready to abandon them!

Stop Looking to Prove Yourself Right
– Jay Baer, author, speaker, Founder of Convince & Convert

A while ago, after we had been doing fairly well with the online newsletter, we decided it was time to change direction. We believed the newsletter could be better. So we completely reformatted it and changed the focus of it to help people with the kinds of content they really needed. We did look at the numbers and, while we were growing, we knew where we wanted to be wasn't where we were headed in terms of the types of content, format of content, style, daily notifications. So we made a decision to scrap what we were doing in order to go in a direction that we thought would be better in the long run. And it was really, really scary.

I mean *really scary*. We had paid sponsors and we were essentially pulling the rug out from what we were doing. We were starting over in a new direction and, though we believed ultimately it was the right thing to do, there was a lot of short-term anxiety. We didn't know if sponsors would come back. Many of them thankfully did. It was a frightening time.

My big lesson here: definitely do the research and be willing to prove yourself wrong. That's not how most of us are wired. We don't seek out information that proves ourselves wrong. Going with your gut is important as long as you have done the research. Numbers matter.

Prepare and Listen to Your Gut
– Bryan Kramer, author, speaker, Partner in PureMatter Agency

I was preparing for my TED talk in 2015. I had my TED talk scripted down to the word because that's what the TED committee expects. Yet, I am not a scripted guy at all.

I gave the talk in rehearsal in front of my coach, TED personnel including the producer of the event and my wife, and she knows me. I came across stodgy, stuck, stiff and it did not feel right at all. In fact, it was the worst presentation delivery ever.

My wife looked at me and at the producer and then, in that moment, everyone got it. I am not a script person.

We literally ripped up the script and I let out a big sigh of relief. And I didn't practice that night before the talk, and things flowed so much easier and more smoothly.

Had I stood up for what I knew was right earlier, I would have saved months of heartache. Although I am glad I did the talk, I am very glad I eventually listened to my gut as did others, and we shifted gears.

That experience made me a better speaker. It went way beyond the talk. It changed the way I speak. I now start with the end story and then give the detail and backstory leading up to that.

Prepare and Roll with the Unexpected Shit
– Rene Siegel, Founder & President of High Tech Connect

If you do your homework and prepare well in advance, the crazy, unexpected shit won't derail you. Good preparation makes the improvisation easier, I guess!

I don't do improv but if you're not up on current events, you're screwed, right? I had to present to 8 VPs of a $6B tech company at their 5th Avenue Manhattan office. My husband (minority share owner) and I flew to do the presentation.

But it was 90 degrees with 90% humidity. And there was a taxi strike.

So we had to walk 10 city blocks from our hotel to the meeting. My new Nike/Cole Haan patent peep-toe pumps were too big and despite Kleenex shoved inside, I could NOT walk in them. I literally shuffled 10 blocks.

We finally arrived and waited in the lobby. I looked over to see my hubby's shirt was soaked in sweat. He wore a sport coat, but the entire front was dark from sweat. And when the client came to get us, I awkwardly shuffled my too-big shoes into the conference room and glared at my hubby to button his sport coat. It didn't matter. We both looked wilted and when the projector connector didn't work, I stalled with chit-chat and a giant box of chocolates, while hubby valiantly rebooted the crusty old projector and got it to recognize our laptop.

Would you believe that absolute CLUSTER helped me? I was so mortified by what had happened on the way, I just delivered my presentation with less pressure on me. I was already in oh-what-the-hell-we're-not-going-to-get-it-anyway mode, so I presented and answered questions with a greater sense of calm.

Believe it or not, we landed the new client and became their sole agency for all marketing collateral for several years, from 3000 miles away.

My big lesson: always prepare and also know that the unexpected will happen. Don't work hard and then be derailed by that. Roll with whatever unexpected stuff comes your way.

Be Vulnerable For the Right Reasons
– Jennifer LeBlanc, Founder of ThinkResults Marketing

The very first time I went "off script" in my speaking was the speech I did on fear for Women in Consulting (WiC). I made a really big decision to "go there" – to get vulnerable in order to connect. Here I am talking about taking big bold risks and how can I do that and be closed off? So I shared the personal details of how my divorce left me incredibly financially insecure. Talk about fear.

The sharing of my financial situation following my divorce when I didn't have enough money to buy much food for several months was very, very hard to share. I remember being so nervous telling it.

I did it anyway because I could feel the audience was trying to connect to working through the fear and I was calling them to live more boldly. I had to be bold or I had no credibility. And the connection and stories I heard from others who were so relieved to have their similar experiences validated was totally worth the sharing my darkest moments in public.

The thing is my sharing was relevant to the topic. It was contextually appropriate and I could feel that. My big lesson: be bold. When you are vulnerable and "go there" for the right reasons – to help others, to connect – good things will happen because of it.

THE END

ENDNOTES

[i] http://contentmarketinginstitute.com/wp-content/uploads/2015/09/2016_B2B_Report_Final.pdf

[ii] https://www.youtube.com/watch?v=9X0weDMh9C4

[iii] http://www.blogtalkradio.com/kathyklotzguest/2015/11/05/story-spine-simple-model-for-business-storytelling

[iv] http://keepingithuman.com/art-of-business-storytelling-a-simple-model/

[v] https://www.linkedin.com/pulse/forget-fairy-tale-story-successful-marketing-starts-ends-klotz-guest?trk=hp-feed-article-title-share

[vi] http://www.slideshare.net/fred.zimny/ceb-2013-paper-from-promotion-to-emotion-connecting-b2b-customers-to-brands

[vii] http://www.neurosciencemarketing.com/blog/articles/emotional-ads-work-best.htm#sthash.yu8l31Jn.dpuf

[viii] https://www.flickr.com/photos/robnas/

[ix] https://digest.bps.org.uk/2013/03/20/the-scourge-of-meeting-late-comers/

[x] https://www.youtube.com/c/KathyKlotzGuest

[xi] https://www.flickr.com/photos/visualpunch/

[xii] https://vimeo.com/92823193

[xiii] https://www.youtube.com/watch?v=hFN2AuJC8_k

[xiv] https://www.linkedin.com/pulse/jam-nooice-what-key-peele-can-teach-powerful-content-klotz-guest?trk=mp-author-card

[xv] https://www.linkedin.com/pulse/how-john-olivers-team-creates-content-gets-shared-hell-klotz-guest?trk=prof-post

[xvi] http://www.npr.org/2012/09/05/160643183/transcript-bill-clintons-convention-speech

[xvii] http://www.cmo.com/features/articles/2015/12/2/2016-predictions.html#gs.kZ6YgbA

Plea for Support: Help Me Make My Next Book Better

Please leave a helpful REVIEW on Amazon

To receive special extras such as behind the scenes and how-to videos, and articles, email me a copy of your book receipt (kathy@keepingithuman.com) with the words "extras please" in the subject line, and I'll add you to the list. Thank you for getting the book and giving it your time. I appreciate your feedback, and I love hearing what you have to say. Your input will help make the next edition better and make my mom feel like I've done something useful with my life. So, everybody wins.

You could be featured in my next book

Email me your results so I can make the next book even better. When you do, you and your business *could be* featured in my next book.

Thank you!
Kathy Klotz-Guest
@kathyklotzguest
Kathy@keepingithuman.com

ABOUT THE AUTHOR

Kathy Klotz-Guest, MA, MBA, MLA, is a business storytelling strategist, facilitator, speaker, and funny lady. Founder of Keeping it Human, her mission is to help organizations turn jargon-monoxide into compelling stories and uncover boldly creative ideas for marketing content, products, branding and more (idea orgasms!). A podcaster and comic improviser, Kathy has written two other short books on humor, content, and storytelling (*The Executive's Bedtime Guide* series) in addition to *Stop Boring Me!* Her work has been published in *Convince and Convert*, *Business of Story*, *Marketing Profs*, *Ragan.com*, *PR Daily*, *Business2Community*, and *Customer Think*. Her 7-year-old is still her favorite audience to make laugh.

CPSIA information can be obtained
at www.ICGtesting.com
Printed in the USA
FFHW02n0235110918
48225340-51960FF

9 781684 191093